Three African Visionaries

Nkrumah

Nyerere

Senghor

Lawrence E.K. Lupalo

Three African Visionaries: Nkrumah, Nyerere, Senghor

First Edition

ISBN-13: 978-1535596114
ISBN-10: 1535596112

CreateSpace
Scotts Valley, California, USA

Kwame Nkrumah

Julius Nyerere

Leopold Sédar Senghor

Introduction

THIS WORK looks at three African visionaries –
Nkrumah, Nyerere and Senghor – and the paths they felt
the continent should take in its quest for unity and
development; how it should define and foster its identity;
and what role it should play in the international arena as an
integral part of the global community.

It also explores some of the differences they had in
pursuit of those goals.

The book is not intended to be an in-depth analysis or a
scholarly work on the three leaders. Instead, it is intended
to be a simple introduction to some of the things they did
and the goals they pursued.

The three leaders will be remembered for their
innovative ways in their attempts to chart a new course for
Africa after the end of colonial rule. And they all had their
successes and failures.

Nyerere will be remembered for the big role he played
in the liberation of the countries of southern Africa which
were still under white minority rule. He will also be
remembered for his massive experiment in social
engineering, unprecedented in the continent's post-colonial
history, when he tried to restructure Tanzania by

establishing communal villages – known as *ujamaa* villages – across the country in his quest to transform the country into a socialist society.

One of Nyerere's critics and admirers, renowned Kenyan professor, Ali Mazrui, described Nyerere in the following terms: "He was one of the giants of the 20th century....He did bestride this narrow world like an African colossus."

Nkrumah was another African colossus. He also stood out in his own way.

More than any other African leader, Nkrumah was the embodiment of immediate continental unification to create a United States of Africa under one government. There was no other leader who was as vocal and as passionate as he was in pursuit of that goal.

In fact, he was in a class by himself, and lonely, in his desire to see African countries united under one government immediately or as soon as possible; a vision most of his colleagues did not share.

Those who agreed with him on the need for a united Africa felt that African countries would not be able to unite right away under one government when there was not even an attempt to form an exploratory committee under the auspices of the Organisation of African Unity (OAU) to chart the course towards unification. They saw Nkrumah's quest for immediate continental unification as no more than a dream and an unrealistic goal.

Still, there was an imperative need for unity. As Nyerere stated in his speech in Accra, Ghana, during Ghana's 40th independence anniversary:

"After Kwame Nkrumah was removed from the African political scene nobody took up the challenge again....Without unity, there is no future for Africa."

Although Nyerere is best remembered as the leader who carried out the most ambitious, most radical and far-reaching exercise in social engineering on the entire continent during the post-colonial era when he tried to transform Tanzania into a socialist society through his policy of *ujamaa*, it is his enduring legacy as one of the strongest and relentless supporters of the liberation movements in southern Africa which earned him a place in the pantheon of African leadership spanning centuries.

During his leadership, Tanzania was the headquarters of all the African liberation movements. It also harboured guerrilla camps for training freedom fighters from the countries of southern Africa which were still under white minority rule.

Both Nkrumah and Nyerere were the embodiment of Pan-Africanism during a period when optimism for Africa's future was at its peak and the spirit of unity resonated across the continent. They are still symbols of what Africa can and should be in terms of unity, equality and development.

With regard to African identity, it was Senghor who added a controversial dimension to it with his concept of *négritude*; an assertion and affirmation of black identity that has been hailed and ridiculed through the years by some Africans and non-Africans alike. What is *négritude*? Critics ask. Some of them have even tried to answer the question in their attempt to dismiss the concept as something hollow, meaningless, and irrelevant.

Nigerian writer Wole Soyinka dismissed it condescendingly when he said, "A tiger does not proclaim its tigritude."

French philosopher Jean Paul Satre hailed *négritude* as "anti-racist racism," as did Senghor himself, a paradoxical compliment that continues to stimulate and fuel debate on this philosophy and intellectual movement started by black intellectuals in Paris, in the very heart and soul of the colonial power that was ruling their countries during their lifetime.

They came from Africa and the Caribbean – mainly

Martinique. And they together asserted their humanity by proclaiming pride in their identity as black people who had a common African ancestry, with a proud history and civilisation, which was no less noble than that of their conquerors.

To these three thinkers, Africa owes a lot as her people continue to seek answers to questions about the future of their motherland.

Where are we headed as a people? What is our destiny? Do we really know? Is our future as Africans shrouded in mystery? President Ahmed Sekou Toure – a staunch Pan-Africanist in the same league with Nkrumah, Nyerere, Lumumba and a few others – once said even the shape of Africa is a question mark in reverse. Yet he knew exactly where he wanted Africa to go.

Do we?

Lawrence E.K. Lupalo
Dar es Salaam, Tanzania
29 July 2016

Three African Visionaries:
What Africa Should Be

Kwame Nkrumah, Julius Nyerere and Leopold Sédar Senghor were some of the most prominent leaders and thinkers in the history of post-colonial Africa.

They shared a vision of a united Africa. But they differed on how to achieve that goal. Also, they pursued socialism. But they differed on what kind of socialism to pursue, although they agreed on the fundamental principles which form the basis of socialism. Also, there was one major difference between Senghor and the other two leaders.

Although Senghor was known to be a proponent of African socialism like Nyerere and was critical of capitalism saying it was against African traditional values of communal living and sharing, he was not really a socialist; nor did he genuinely try to implement any form of socialism leading to radical transformation of society when he was president of Senegal. He was also strongly anti-Marxist.

Nkrumah, on the other hand, was a Marxist-Leninist. Nyerere was an African socialist and probably the strongest proponent of African socialism.

The three leaders are also known for their vision of Africa: what path Africa as a continent should take towards development; what kind of identity it should have; and what place Africans should have in the international arena in relation to other members of the global community.

But in spite of this shared vision, or the different visions the three leaders had in terms of Africa's place and role in the international community, there were fundamental differences among them.

Senghor was a Francophile and unabashedly pro-Western in spite of his professions of Africanity and African socialism.

Nkrumah wanted to implement Marxism adapted to African conditions but downplayed the Leninist aspect of his political philosophy, although he was strongly influenced by Leninism as much as he was by Marxism.

Among the three leaders, it was only Nyerere who was genuinely committed to the pursuit of African socialism. He was also critical of those who believed that socialism could be achieved only through Marxism. Nkrumah was one of them.

Professor Ali Mazrui described Nkrumah as a Leninist Czar. As he stated in his article, "Nkrumah: The Leninist Czar," in *Transition*, a scholarly magazine published in Kampala in the sixties, founded and edited by Rajat Neogy when Mazrui was a professor of political science at Makerere:

"Kwame Nkrumah's first important publication twenty years ago was inspired by Lenin's theory of imperialism. The publication came to be entitled *Towards Colonial Freedom*. Nkrumah's last publication in office is his new book, *Neo-Colonialism: The Last Stage of Imperialism*. That too owes its doctrinal inspiration to Lenin's theory of imperialism.

There is little doubt that, quite consciously, Nkrumah

saw himself as an African Lenin. He wanted to go down in history as a major political theorist – and he wanted a particular stream of thought to bear his own name. Hence the term 'Nkrumahism' – a name for an ideology that he hoped would assume the same historic and revolutionary status as 'Leninism.' The fountainhead of both Nkrumahism and Leninism was to remain Marxism – but these two streams that flowed from Marx were to have a historic significance in their own right.

Like Lenin, Nkrumah created 'the Circle' – a group of friends to discuss ideas and formulate theories of revolution. Like Lenin, Nkrumah encouraged the emergence of a Marxist newspaper called *Spark*. It is true that *The Spark* in Ghana came to be more purist in its Marxism than Nkrumah himself. Nevertheless, the idea of such a newspaper was directly inspired by *Iskra* (Spark), the Marxist paper which was founded in 1901 through Lenin's initiative.

But while Nkrumah strove to be Africa's Lenin, he also sought to become Ghana's Czar. Nor is Nkrumah's Czarism necessarily 'the worse side' of his personality and behaviour. On the contrary, his Czarism could – in moderation – have mitigated some of the harshness of his Leninism. It is even arguable that a Leninist Czar was what a country like Ghana needed for a while.

Nkrumah's tragedy was a tragedy of *excess*, rather than of contradiction. He tried to be too much of a revolutionary monarch." - (Ali A. Mazrui, "Nkrumah: The Leninist Czar," *Transition*, Kampala, Uganda, 1966, p. 26).

Nkrumah also tried very hard to be acknowledged as a top-notch intellectual and as a philosopher instead of waiting to be accorded such status; hence his claim to Nkrumahism that would immortalise him as one of the world's great political thinkers. Unfortunately, he was not. He tried to study for a doctorate in philosophy at the

University of London but dropped out. His supervisor in the doctoral programme said Nkrumah was not really a philosopher and did not have an analytical mind.

He was an average intellectual but very passionate, charismatic, dynamic, militant, daring, and outspoken on African and international affairs; attributes which, together with his forceful personality and oratorical skills, thrust him into the international spotlight and kept him there throughout his political career.

Nkrumah's Pan-Africanist mentor, C.L.R. James, in a letter he wrote to George Padmore in 1945 to introduce Nkrumah when Nkrumah moved to London where Padmore was living, bluntly stated: "He is not very bright." But he asked Padmore to help "this young man (who) is coming to you" because he "is determined to throw the Europeans out of Africa."

That is exactly what Nkrumah went on to do when he returned to the Gold Coast (Ghana) in 1947. As he stated in his autobiography about the ambition he had when he was still a student in the United States:

"My first duty is to return to Africa and join in the struggle for its liberation from the tentacles of colonialism."

He was deeply committed to the liberation of Africa and was continentalist in outlook even when he led the struggle for independence in his home country. When the Gold Coast won independence on 6 March 1957 and became Ghana, he declared:

"The independence of Ghana is meaningless unless it is linked with the total liberation of Africa."

C.L.R. James and George Padmore were childhood friends in Trinidad (as Kenneth Kaunda and Simon Kapwewe were, in Chinsali, in the Northern Province,

Northern Rhodesia). Both became giants in the Pan-African movement and enduring symbols of Pan-Africanism. C.L.R. James also taught Eric Williams in secondary school in Trinidad. Eric Williams became the first prime minister of Trinidad and Tobago after the island nation won independence from Britain in 1962.

C.L.R. James also wrote the following about Nkrumah:

"He used to talk a lot about imperialism and Leninism and export capital, and he used to talk a lot of nonsense." – (C.L. R. James, in Tony Martin, *The Pan-African Connection: From Slavery to Garvey and Beyond*, Dover, Massachusetts, USA: The Majority Press, 1983, p. 168. See also C.L. R. James, "Document: C.L.R. James on the Origins," *Radical America*, Vol. II, No. 4, July – August 1968, p. 26, cited by Tony Martin, "C.L.R. James and The Race/Class Question," p. 185).

He said basically the same thing about Jomo Kenyatta. In a lecture as late as 1973, C.L. R. James said the following about Kenyatta:

"At the time (in the 1940s), and even today, he was not very bright."

He also provided the context in which he made those remarks. In his lecture, "Reflections on Pan-Africanism," on 20 November 1973, in which he also talked about Kenyatta, C.L.R. James said the following about Nkrumah:

"Padmore decided to hold a conference in Manchester. He invited them all up and they came. By himself he could never have had that conference (the Fifth Pan-African Congress in 1945)....a very famous conference.
At that conference there was Kenyatta, there was Nkrumah, and there was laid down at this conference the

policy which Nkrumah carried out afterward in the Gold Coast.

Now I have to tell you how Nkrumah got in touch with Padmore and how that organization came to have these two men together. I was in the United States in 1941 and a member of my political organization came to me and told me:

'There is a young African here and he says he would like to see you.' I said, 'Well, why should he say he would like to see me?' 'Well, I told him about you and he has read your book and I told him I could take him to see you and he said his name is Francis Nkrumah.'

So Nkrumah turned up, very neat, very graceful, very assured, he always has been, and we got together and we got to be friendly. And he spent two years with us. We used to go down to Lincoln University in Pennsylvania, he would come up to New York and spend some time with us. We were very close until in 1943 (1945) he said he was going to England to study law and I wrote a letter, a letter that is famous in our annals.

I said, 'Dear George, there is a young African coming to England to study law. He is not very bright, but nevertheless he is determined to throw the imperialists out of Africa. Do what you can for him.'

George met him at Waterloo station and there began that combination.

Now, why did I say that he was not very bright? Nkrumah used to talk about surplus value, capital instead of commodities. He had picked up these from some superficial quarters. He did not understand them really. About two years afterwards I saw Nkrumah and had read an article that he had written on Imperialism. He had learned from Padmore's extensive library and all sorts of papers and clippings. It was fully organized particularly in regard to the colonial policies of the African powers.

And Nkrumah was able to learn and was educated a great deal by Padmore. In addition to that, Nkrumah brought much creative energy and knowledge of Africa and instinctive political development which fortified Padmore and the two of them became a tremendous power together in the movement." – (C.L. R. James, "Reflections on Pan-Africanism," 20 November 1973, C.L. R. James Archive).

Nkrumah was not an original thinker with an analytical mind like Nyerere and Senghor, although he obviously wanted people to think he was one. Nyerere never claimed such distinction even implicitly. It was the people, including his critics, who acknowledged his intellectual power. In fact, he made exactly the same point in a speech at a conference at Diamond Jubilee Hall in Dar es Salaam, Tanzania – the audience included foreign delegates – in 1970 in which he said don't tell people you are intelligent, or even imply you are; let other people say you are.

Even some of Nyerere's critics who also admired him because of his astonishing intelligence, high ethical standards, and commitment to African liberation and independence, said he surpassed Senghor in terms of intellectual capacity. As Jonathan Power, a British conservative, stated – when he wrote about Nyerere's high intellectual calibre – in his article, "Lament for Independent Africa's Greatest Leader":

"Measured against most of his peers, Jomo Kenyatta of Kenya, Kwame Nkrumah of Ghana, Ahmed Sekou Toure of Guinea, he towered above them. On the intellectual plane only the rather remote president of Senegal, the great poet and author of Negritude, Leopold Senghor, came close to him." – Jonathan Power, TFF Jonathan Power Columns, "Lament for Independent Africa's Greatest Leader," London, 6 October 1999).

British journalist Trevor Grundy, another critic of Mwalimu Nyerere who once worked in Tanzania – at the *Standard*, renamed *Daily News*, Dar es Salaam – from 1968 to 1972, wrote the following about Nyerere's intellectual capacity:

"He went on to use his Edinburgh years to great advantage, bewildering (some might say bamboozling) liberal-minded journalists in the 1960s and 1970s with his formidable intellect....

He had a blotting paper brain. Hardly a soul at Edinburgh guessed he would turn into Africa's number one brain box in years to come....Statesmen and journalists were amazed at his knowledge....The Rhodesian leader Ian Smith several times referred to Nyerere as Africa's 'evil genius.'"

Professor Mazrui, who said Nyerere was the most intellectual African leader, also stated the following in an interview with *The Gambia Echo*, 25 July 2008:

"The fact that Nkrumah had a greater positive impact on me than has any other leader does not necessarily mean that I admire Nkrumah the most. Intellectually, I admired Julius K. Nyerere of Tanzania higher than most politicians anywhere in the world. Nyerere and I also met more often over the years from 1967 to 1997 approximately."

Among African leaders, Nyerere was in a class by himself as a formidable intellectual, unlike Nkrumah.

There are also questions about the authorship of some of Nkrumah's works. The renowned Ghanaian philosopher, Dr. Willie Abraham who wrote *The Mind of Africa*, a highly acclaimed philosophical text, helped Nkrumah write some of his books, including *Consciencism: Philosophy and ideology for decolonization and development with particular reference to the African*

18

Revolution which was first published in April 1964, about two years before Nkrumah was overthrown in February 1966.

In fact, he is the one who wrote the book. When the book first came out, there were whispers, right away, saying Dr. Willie Abraham was the one who wrote it; only to be confirmed later that he was indeed the one who did.

At the book's launch in Accra, Ghana, on 2 April 1964, and in Nkrumah's presence, Dr. Willie Abraham said among other things:

"Kwame Nkrumah has spoken time and again of the un-flowering of the African genius in conditions of independence. In this unflowering, he is himself making a contribution that is already astonishing. He has already proved himself a strategist, a thinker, and a statesman. Now, by his book *Consciencism*, he establishes himself firmly as a philosopher....In *Consciencism,* he has at length presented us with the matrix and theoretical sanction of his practice.

Consciencism opens with a discussion of philosophy. The author admits that it is possible to look at philosophy in diverse ways, but singles out two ways of treating it for extended development. The first which occupies the first chapter of the book is called by him the academic treatment. This, he says, arises from an attitude to philosophy as if there were 'nothing to them but statements standing in logical relation to one another.'

What this means is that the conclusions and the purpose of philosophical utterance are in this treatment made of less significance than the logical connections between the sentences. A whole philosophy can through being treated like this be made to hang in thin air having no connection with anything concrete or consequential. Philosophy thus becomes a kind of parlour-game, a mere intellectual jousting.

To develop philosophy like this, Kwame Nkrumah

could have used the plain historical method, moving from philosopher to philosopher. This would have been excessively laborious, repetitious and without much profit. His method was instead to identify the basic questions of philosophy, and to follow these questions through the characteristic treatment given to them by academic philosophy.

These questions are identified by Kwame Nkrumah as the question 'what there is' and the question how 'what there is' might be explained. If these are the basic questions of philosophy, then the answers to them must already determine the character of the entire philosophy of man. When such a claim is made, it is naturally needful to substantiate it. The claim gains substantiation in both the first and the fourth chapters; but especially in the fourth chapter where the author painstakingly shows how step by step his own answers to the two questions determine his ethical, political, and epistemological position.

Still developing the academic treatment, Kwame Nkrumah divides answers to the first question according to their treatment of matter. Those which accord to matter an absolute and independent existence, he groups together as materialism. And with this group he contrasts idealism.

Always going to the root of the matter, he avoids for the time being a headlong engagement with idealism, until he has identified its sources. These he finds in solipsism and in a theory of perception. He distinguishes two stages of solipsism, complete and incipient. I quote part of his discussion of complete solipsism:

'In complete solipsism the individual is identified with the universe. The universe comes to consist of the individual and his experience. And when we seek to inquire a little of what this gigantic individual who fills the universe is compounded, we are confronted with diverse degrees of incoherence. In solipsism, the individual starts from a depressing scepticism about the existence of other people and other things. While in the grip of this pessimism, he pleasantly ignores the fact that his own body is part of that external world, that he sees and touches his own body in exactly the same sense that he sees and touches any other body. If other bodies are only portions of the individual's experience, then by the same magic he must disincarnate himself. In this way, the individual's role as the centre of solipsism begins to wobble seriously, he is no longer the peg on which the universe hangs, the hub around which it revolves. Solipsism begins to shed its focal point for the universe. The individual begins to coalesce with his own experience. The individual as a subject, the sufferer and enjoyer of experience, melts away, and we are left with unattached experience.'

This passage is one of many which illustrate the author's succinctness of expression and vividness of thought. It is from this combination added to the accuracy of exposition and cogency of argument that consciencism derives its power.

Incipient solipsism is illustrated from the philosophy of Descartes. Kwame Nkrumah argues that when Descartes proposes to doubt everything that could be known through the senses or through reasoning, because both avenues of knowledge are full of pit-falls, and decides that he who is busy doubting things must exist in order to doubt, and therefore claims to exist, he claims too much. And now I quote:

'Though Descartes is entitled to say: *Cogito, ergo sum* – 'I think therefore I exist' – he would clearly be understanding too much if he understood from this that some object existed, let alone Monsieur Descartes existed. All that is indubitable in the first section of Descartes' statement is that there is thinking. The first person is in that statement no more than the subject of a verb, with no more connotation of an object than there is in the anticipatory 'it' of the sentence 'It is raining.' The pronoun in this sentence is a mere subject of a sentence, and does not refer to any object or group of objects which is raining. 'It' in that sentence does not stand for anything. It is a quack pronoun.

And so once again we have unattached experience, thinking without an object which thinks.

And as the subject is merely grammatical, it cannot serve as a genuine principle of collection of thoughts which will mark one batch of thoughts as belonging to one person rather than another...'

Discussing the other source of solipsism, Kwame Nkrumah writes:

'It is more normal to found idealism upon some theory of perception. Here, the idealist holds that we only know of the external world through perception; and if matter be held to be constitutive of the external world, then we only know of matter through perception. Quite gratuitously, the conclusion is drawn that matter owes its existence to perception. Granted that perception is a function of the mind or spirit, matter ends up depending on spirit for its existence.'

The author goes on to point out that the conception of perception involved is one which takes place by agency of our senses. And as our bodies are themselves parts of the external world, if body, being matter, exists only through perceptual knowledge, 'it could not at the same time be the means to that knowledge; it could not be the avenue to perception'....

Kwame Nkrumah does not content himself with attacking idealism at its roots. He also seeks to establish that idealism is jejune; that it cannot explain anything, and that it is incompatible with science and the existence of ordinary things like apples and oranges. His reason is that the idealists dismantle the world, and find that they cannot put it together again....

There are two aspects of the philosophical materialism of *Consciencism*. In its first aspect, it is a combative theory, seeking to destroy philosophical idealism to which it stands opposed. In its second aspect, it is ampliative. It seeks to give a general philosophical account of the world in exactly the same way as idealism is ampliative. Hence *Consciencism* not merely denies the theses of idealism: it substitutes for them its own theses.

Consciencism describes idealism variously as 'intoxicated speculation' and 'the ecstasy of intellectualism.'

In contrast, materialism is sober philosophy. The initial theses of materialism, according to *Consciencism*, are first the absolute and independent existence of matter; and second the assertion of the capacity of matter for spontaneous self-motion. And yet *Consciencism* criticises materialism...."

Dr. Willie Abraham was talking about himself, and about his own book, not about Nkrumah and Nkrumah's book. Excerpts from *Consciencism* make that clear. Those who knew Nkrumah well knew, right away, that was not even his language and reasoning. He was not known for such philosophical profundity like Dr. Willie Abraham. That was not even his writing style. There is a big difference between the excerpts above – from the book, *Consciencism* – and Nkrumah's own writings in terms of style, substance, and reasoning.

If Nkrumah had a reputation for such intellectual depth, he definitely would have been able to formulate his own philosophy and ideology, based on his own original ideas, instead of relying on Marxism-Leninism as the basis for Nkrumahism – which was no more than an African name for scientific socialism, the intellectual product of

Karl Marx more than anybody else – in a futile attempt to indiginise or Africanise Marxism.

Simply known as the mighty Abraham in some circles because of his formidable intellect, Dr. Willie Abraham was very close to Nkrumah and was the intellectual force behind a philosophy club founded by Nkrumah. He was also the club's leading philosophical theorist. In fact, he was Nkrumah's court philosopher and was brutalised by the new military rulers after Nkrumah was overthrown. Born in May 1934, he was almost 32 years old when Nkrumah was ousted and was vice chancellor of the University of Ghana during that time.

In the theoretical realm, Nkrumah's writings are a repetition of Marxist arguments and analysis so common among Marxists despite his attempt to formulate his own philosophy which would be distinctly his and reflective of African realities and relevant to African conditions. He was not an intellectual lightweight. But he lacked theoretical insights which would have enabled him to formulate and develop such a philosophy.

Even after years of refinement by its adherents – Kwame Ture being foremost among them – and their attempts to define it, Nkrumahism remains a nebulous concept.

What is Nkrumahism? What are its underlying principles and essential elements *as an original philosophy and ideology*?

Even those who profess to be Nkrumahists have a hard time trying to define it and identify it as a distinct philosophy and ideology except in general terms as a collection of Nkrumah's thoughts and ideas which collectively constitute a philosophy and an ideology called Nkrumahism for the establishment of a socioeconomic and political system of continental relevance. Yet its underlying principles are no more than scientific socialism enunciated by Marx and Engels, repeated by Nkrumah. Without scientific socialism, there would be no

Nkruhamism. Therefore, without Marx and Engels, and without Lenin, whose ideas inspired Nkrumah, there would be no Nkrumahism. And there would be no Nkrumah as a socialist thinker.

What would he be, as "an original thinker," without scientific socialism or if he had never even heard of it since that is what formed the foundation of "his own" philosophy?

Kofi Baako, one of Nkrumah's most trusted lieutenants who served as Leader of the House and Minister of State for Parliamentary Affairs and who also was the ruling party's ideologue – of the Convention People's Party (CPP) – put it "succinctly" when he defined Nkrumaism in an attempt to give it a distinct character in his article, "Nkrumaism – Its Theory and Practice," published in *The Party*, CPP Journal, Accra, 1961:

"I would define Nkrumaism as a nonatheistic socialist philosophy which seeks to apply the current socialist ideas to the solution(s) of our problems – be they domestic or international – by adapting these ideas to the realities of our everyday life. It is basically socialism adapted to suit the conditions and circumstances of Africa." – Kofi Baako, "Nkrumaism – Its Theory and Practice," in *The Party*, CPP Journal, Accra, Nos. 4 – 7, April, May, June and July, 1961; reprinted in Paul E. Sigmund, Jr., ed., *The Ideologies of the Developing Nations*, New York: Frederick A. Praeger, New York, 1963, p. 188; see also pp. 188 – 196. See also Kofi Baako, in Ebenezer Obiri Addo, *Kwame Nkrumah: A Case Study of Religion and Politics in Ghana*, Lanham, New York, Oxford: University Press of America, Inc., 1997, p. 159, when he made a futile attempt to define Nkrumaism as a distinct ideology in his address to Ghanaian envoys on 4 February 1962).

The last statement itself is a concession that the socialist ideas Kofi Baako wrote about did not come from

25

Africa.

A staunch Nkrumaist who worked with Nkrumah right from the beginning when they and their other colleagues including Komla Gbedemah formed the Convention People's Party (CPP) in 1949, Kofi Baako was an avowed socialist who played a critical role in the formation of the CPP.

It was he who mobilised the youth to form a group which became the nucleus of the CPP, around which the party was formed. For that alone, he may even be credited for being the "founding father" of the Convention People's Party which led Ghana to independence and in pursuit of a socialist agenda; although it was Nkrumah's idea to form the party when he left the United Gold Coast Convention (UGCC) where he served as secretary-general; with Komla Gbedemah being acclaimed as the best CPP campaigner and mobiliser especially when Nkrumah was in prison.

The question is: Where did the socialist ideas Kofi Baako was talking about come from?

The socialism he was talking about came from Europe, ideas conceived by Karl Marx, unsuited to African conditions. That was in sharp contrast with Nyerere's socialism which was indigenous and suited to African conditions.

So, what made those ideas – from Europe – Nkrumaist? Why would they constitute Nkrumaism as a philosophy and as an ideology when they were not Nkrumah's original ideas?

Mere application of those ideas, even successfully, does not give legitimacy to the claim by Nkrumaists that it was a Nkrumaist ideology. It is the origin of ideas which gives an ideology a distinct character and identity. If they were Nyerere's, they would be Nyerereist. If they were Nkrumah's, they would be Nkrumaist. If they were Mao's, they would be Maoist. If they were Marx's, they would be Marxist – as they indeed were in this case.

26

Nkrumahism was a product of Marxism and Leninism, not of Nkrumah's own original ideas; hence Nkrumah's own admission that he was a Marxist and scientific socialist, unlike Nyerere who did not seek or get inspiration – and ideas – from outside Africa to formulate his own philosophy and ideology of African socialism known as *ujamaa*.

No other African leader attempted to do what Nyerere did in Tanzania – radically restructure society along socialist lines, including relocating large numbers of people in order to build ujamaa villages. Yet he did not – nor did anybody else in official circles – call this policy, Nyerereism, or a Nyerereist philosophy or ideology.

Also, there were other leaders who adopted Marxism-Leninism the way Nkrumah did. Yet they did not appropriate it and name it after themselves, except Nkrumah who called it Nkrumahism (or Nkrumaism).

Nkrumah's ideological compatriots, Ahmed Sekou Toure of Guinea and Modibo Keita of Mali tried to implement Marxism suited to local conditions. Yet they did not rename it after themselves. It was not called Toureism or a Toureist ideology and philosophy in Guinea; nor was it called Keitaism or Keitaist in Mali.

Mengistu Haile Mariam tried it in Ethiopia. He did not call it Mengistuism or Mariamism. Mathieu Kerekou tried it in Benin. Yet he did not call it Kerekouism. Samora Machel in Mozambique did not call the Marxism-Leninism he tried to implement – Samorist or Machelist. It was only Nkrumah who renamed the Marxism-Leninism he was trying to implement in Ghana – Nkrumaism (or Nkrumahism).

It is also true that socialism was the preferred ideology in many African countries soon after they won independence. Almost all the countries which tried to implement socialism adopted some form of Marxism or Leninism, except Tanzania under Nyerere. As Professor Mazrui stated in his book, *Towards a Pax Africana: A*

Study of Ideology and Ambition:

"No ideology commands respect so widely in Africa as the ideology of 'socialism' – though, as in Europe, it is socialism of different shades.

In Guinea and Mali a Marxist framework of reasoning is evident. In Ghana Leninism was wedded to notions of traditional collectivism. In Tanzania the concept of *Ujamaa*, derived from the sense of community of tribal life, is being radicalized into an assertion of modern socialism.

In Kenya there is a dilemma between establishing socialism and Africanizing the capitalism which already exists. In Nigeria, Senegal and Uganda some kind of allegiance is being paid to the ideal of social justice in situations with a multi-party background.

There are places, of course, where no school of socialism is propagated at all. But outside the Ivory Coast there is little defiant rejection of the idea of 'socialism' in former colonial Africa." – (Ali A. Mazrui, *Towards a Pax Africana: A Study of Ideology and Ambition*, London: Weidenfeld and Nicolson, 1967, p. 97. Cited by A. Mazrui, see also William H. Friedland and Carl G. Rosberg, Jr., eds., *African Socialism*, Stanford: Stanford University Press, 1964; Kenneth W. Grundy, "Marxism-Leninism: The Mali Approach, *International Journal*, Vol. XVII, No. 3, Summer 1962; L. Gray Cowan, "Guinea," in Gwendolen M. Carter, ed., *African One-Party States*, Ithaca, New York: Cornell University Press, 1962; Kenneth W. Grundy, "Nkrumah's Theory of Underdevelopment: An Analysis of Recurrent Themes," *World Politics*, Vol. XV, No. 3, April 1963; Kenya Government Paper, *African Socialism and Its Application to Planning in Kenya*, 1965; *Africa Report*, Special issue on African Socialism, VIII, May 1963.

No other African leader tried to implement an

indigenous form of socialism the way Nyerere did, despite professions even by capitalist-oriented leaders such as Tom Mboya that African socialism was real and was the only form of socioeconomic system that was best for Africa. They did not go as far as Nyerere did, yet acknowledged the existence of socialism or socialist elements in traditional societies across the continent. As Mboya stated in *Transition*, Kampala, November 1963:

"I have not suggested that we have to go delving into the past seeking socialism. It is a continuing tradition among our people. Does the writer of the letter think that socialism had to be given a name before it became a reality? It is an attitude towards people practised in our societies and did not need to be codified into a scientific theory in order to find existence." – (Tom Mboya, *Transition*, Vol. 3, No. 11, November 1963, p. 6, cited by A.A. Mazrui, ibid., pp. 101, and 262).

Mboya was responding to a critic, C. N. Omondi, who wrote a letter to the editor, *Transition*, questioning the validity of the claim that socialism was indigenous to Africa. Omondi's letter was first published in *Kenya Weekly*, 2 August 1963.

In spite of Mboya's spirited defence of the existence of socialism in traditional societies across Africa, there is no question that socialism, in any form, was never practised in his home country, Kenya, as official or unofficial policy even when he was minister of economic planning. Among all African leaders, it was Nyerere who became the most articulate exponent and theorist of African socialism and its most consistent practitioner at the national level.

Nyerere said people in traditional societies across Africa lived on the basis of socialist values and principles; yet they had never even heard of Karl Marx. He elevated that to the national level and said we can build modern nations on that basis.

Nkrumah said it had to be done on the basis of scientific socialism – hence Marxism; even if modified to suit African conditions, it still was an alien ideology imported from Europe whose relevance to Africa was questionable even though it inspired Nkrumah. That was the basis for Nkrumahism, also known as Nkrumaism and its exponents as Nkrumaists or Nkrumahists.

Marxism itself is now a discredited ideology, refuted by historical experience, as has been demonstrated by the collapse of communism around the world. Yet Nkrumahism continues to seek sustenance and validity from Marxism.

Nyerere gave an appropriate response to the disciples of Karl Marx and proponents of scientific socialism in the African context when he said Karl Marx was not an infallible divinity. He said Africans don't need to be taught socialism by Karl Marx or by any other scientific socialists – it already existed in traditional societies across the continent.

He went on to explain that it makes no sense to try to build our nations based on what Karl Marx wrote more than 100 years ago and on his analysis of conditions which prevailed in Europe, not in Africa, during his time when we can think for ourselves and find solutions to our problems based on our own analysis of the conditions which exist in our societies today. Nkrumaists say they already have answers – provided by Karl Marx more than 100 years ago.

Nkrumahism as a philosophy and as an ideology can *not* stand on its own as a product of an original thinker – there is nothing original about it. And it has failed to stand the test of time, unlike Marxism and Leninism. It has been shunted into oblivion. It is moribund at best. It may be in the political lexicon of Nkrumahists and a number of other militant or radical Pan-Africanists but hardly as a distinct ideology that is original and uniquely African like *ujamaa* expounded by Nyerere.

Nkrumah himself was not even sure how to proceed in his quest for a doctrine that would define and underlie his political thought that would be distinctly his. As Colin Legum stated in his chapter,"Socialism in Ghana: A Political Interpretation," in *African Socialism*:

"(There were) growing divergences between *The Spark* and Nkrumah, especially during 1963 and the opening months of 1964, (which) have baffled outsiders. But it now seems clear that Nkrumah was deeply engaged in the search for a doctrine of socialism that would be of general application to Africa. His need was to reconcile his own socialist ideas with Pan-Africanism through a philosophy that would establish his position as a messianic leader on the continent.

He wished to do for Africa what Marx and Lenin had done for Europe and Mao Tse-tung for China. While willing to learn from them, he was unwilling to accept their philosophies. He therefore established his own Philosophy Club, with Professor Willie Abraham, a Ghanaian Fellow of All Souls, Oxford, as the main theoretician.

These philosophers, though sympathetic to Marxism, believed that neither the 'scientific socialists' nor the Western philosophers had supplied a doctrine that reflected the needs of Africa: these could come only from an understanding of African society.

Such an approach was not wholly acceptable to *The Spark* Marxists. While they were willing to cloak their 'scientific socialism' in *kente* cloth, they were opposed to thoroughgoing revisionism. They approached Africa entirely through Marxist eyes; the philosophers preferred to approach Marx through African eyes." – (Colin Legum, "Socialism in Ghana: A Political Interpretation," in William H. Friedland and Carl G. Rosberg, eds., *African Socialism*, Stanford, California, USA: Stanford University Press, 1964, p. 155).

Nkrumah himself approached Africa through Marxist eyes although in an attempt to adapt Marxism to African conditions. But the ideology was still Marxist and therefore not Nkrumah's or African. He himself said he was a Marxist even back then and maintained the same position throughout his life. He was *not* an African socialist like Nyerere whose socialist ideas were derived from the African traditional way of life based on the extended family and communal living, not from Marxist interpretations of the dynamics of society across the spectrum.

As a form of scientific socialism, Nkrumahism is irrelevant today, unlike Nyerere's African socialism since socialist elements still exist in traditional societies across the continent. The people in those societies continue to cherish, foster and implement socialist values as they always have throughout our history, especially before the advent of colonial rule.

But Nkrumahism may have legitimacy in the political arena on the basis of three factors associated with Nkrumah: his quest for immediate continental unification, although it was and remains an unattainable ideal; formation of an African high command, first proposed by Nkrumah and which was a more realistic goal; and the concept of neocolonialism, advanced by Nkrumah and validated by experience; although the phenomenon itself – of neocolonialism – had already been discerned by Nyerere as well who, in a speech in Dar es Salaam about three months before Tanganyika's independence in 1961, warned of the Second Scramble for Africa which would take place after African countries emerged from colonial rule.

In fact, Nyerere used the term "neo-imperialism" in June 1960 to describe the same phenomenon Nkrumah did when he coined the term "neocolonialism" later.

Therefore, what was new was *not* the phenomenon but

only the term "neocolonialism" Nkrumah coined to describe it. He probably coined it in 1963, when it was first used, or just before then, while Nyerere used the term "neo-imperialism" three years before then to describe the same phenomenon. As Nyerere stated in June 1960:

"In the struggle against colonialism the fundamental unity of the people of Africa is evident and is deeply felt. It is, however, a unity forged in diversity in a battle against an outside Government.

If the triumph in this battle is to be followed by an equal triumph against the forces of neo-imperialism and also against poverty, ignorance and disease, then this unity must be strengthened and maintained." – (Julius K. Nyerere, "Freedom and Unity," *Transition, Volume 0, Issue 14, 1964*, Kampala, Uganda, pp. 40 – 45. This was a republication of what he wrote earlier in June 1960 before he led Tanganyika to independence the following year. For an analysis of cooperation among the three East African countries of Kenya, Uganda and Tanganyika, see also Donald Rothschild, *Politics of Integration: An East African Documentary*, Nairobi, Kenya: East African Publishing House, 1968).

As a theoretician, Nkrumah did not attain stature comparable to Karl Marx, Lenin and Mao in the global arena as he hoped he would, especially as Africa's "messianic figure." But he was in the same category as Nyerere as one of the world's historical giants. As Professor Mazrui stated in his eulogy of Nyerere: "He was one of the giants of the 20th....He did bestride this narrow world like an African colossus." So did Nkrumah, but not as an original thinker like Nyerere.

Also, Nkrumah did not really write his most controversial book, *Neo-Colonialism: The Last Stage of Imperialism* (published in October 1965), which infuriated American leaders and was one of the reasons they decided to overthrow him.

The book, which was an extension of Lenin's *Imperialism: the Highest Stage of Capitalism*, was actually written by other people although in collaboration with Nkrumah. They included Shirley Graham Du Bois, an African American who was the widow of Dr. W.E. B. Du Bois; Dorothy Pizer, a white British woman who was the partner of George Padmore, Nkrumah's adviser on African affairs; and Hodee Edwards, a white American woman who was a renowned Marxist and who had family ties to the black American community in Accra. Hodee Edwards also worked for the Ghanaian government to provide an intellectual rationale for scientific socialism and refute the validity of African socialism, a position articulated by Abdulrahman Mohamed Babu in the Tanzanian context – outside officialdom.

They all lived in Accra during that period and worked closely with Nkrumah. But Nkrumah's contribution to the book was minimal, in terms of writing, besides supporting the work's central thesis which was elaborated by Hodee Edwards. She played the biggest role in writing the book. Details on the exploitation of Africa by the United States, especially by American corporations, and other facts about the imperial nature of the world's most powerful country came from her; and partly from other pro-Nkrumah Americans such as Shirley Du Bois who was not even allowed to visit the United States to see her friends and relatives soon after Nkrumah was overthrown. She was denied a visa by the American embassy in Accra.

She and her husband moved to Ghana in 1961. They became citizens in 1963 shortly before Dr. W.E.B. Du Bois died. They moved to Ghana at the invitation of Nkrumah. Nkrumah also asked Dr. W.E.B. Du Bois to be the leader of a team that was working on a major project about Africa and the African diaspora: compiling the *Encyclopedia Africana* about the Pan-African world.

Dr. Du Bois is considered by many people in the Pan-

African world to be the father of Pan-Africanism because of the role he played in organising Pan-African conferences and championing the cause of African independence. Nkrumah and Nnamdi Azikiwe were among the people he inspired when they were students in the United States. He died in Accra in August 1963 and was buried there. He was 95 years old.

Had he lived longer, it is possible he could have moved to Tanzania and become a Tanzanian with his wife after Nkrumah was overthrown and replaced by a regime that was hostile to them because of their support for him. Tanzania was held in high esteem by many people in the Pan-African world and elsewhere because of Nyerere's leadership but also incurred the wrath of the imperial powers because of its anti-imperialist stance.

The refusal by the American authorities to allow Shirley Du Bois to go to the United States showed their hostility towards those who supported Nkrumah. Also, the decision by the Du Boises to renounce their American citizenship was not well-received by the American leaders; it was considered to be an insult to them and their great country.

The problems Shirley Du Bois faced when she tried to get a visa to visit the land of her birth, where she had lived her entire life before moving to Ghana, also showed the extent to which the United States was willing to go to punish Nkrumah's allies and supporters.

She even became a citizen of Tanzania and travelled on a Tanzanian passport. But that did not help her enter the United States. The United States did not have very good relations with Tanzania. Also Nyerere, like Sekou Toure, was known to be a strong supporter of Nkrumah. He even offered him asylum but Nkrumah decided to go to Guinea. Nyerere also strongly condemned the coup against Nkrumah when he spoke at a press conference in Dar es Salaam about Nkrumah's ouster.

Nyerere and Nkrumah were also greatly admired by

many black Americans (African Americans) and had basically the same attitude towards the United States as an imperial power which wanted to dominate Africa. About 10 years after Nkrumah was overthrown, Shirley Du Bois, who greatly admired Nyerere as much as she did Nkrumah, even wrote a book about Nyerere, *Julius K. Nyerere: Teacher of Africa*, published in 1975. As Professor Gerald Horne stated in his book, R*ace Woman: The Lives of Shirley Graham Du Bois*, about the problems Mrs. Du Bois had with the American authorities:

"Weeks before the coup (against Nkrumah and which was engineered by the United States), she applied for a thirty-day visa to visit the United States, noting that she had not been to the 'land of my birth' since October 1961, but now she wanted to 'visit my brothers in California, friends in the New York area,' and others...Her visa was denied....

In 1970 she and David (her son) had gone to the Ghanaian embassy in Cairo to renew her passport; unfortunately, they 'were received with extreme discourtesy.' By this point Kwame Nkrumah, who initially had been seen as a virtual co-leader of Guinea with Sekou Toure, was old news; she concluded with sadness that 'it would appear' that Nkrumah 'no longer has any influence where he is,' so a Guinean passport seemed out of the question.

Eventually she was to obtain a Tanzanian passport, but this nation did not have ideal relations with Washington either.

Ultimately she was to receive a visa to return to the United States, but not without considerable lobbying and protest. She returned to a land that in some ways seemed light years away from the nation she had departed only a few years earlier....U.S. authorities were worried that 'a refusal of a visa to Mrs. Du Bois might lead to adverse reaction in certain African nations as well as in the U.S.'" -

(Gerald Horne, R*ace Woman: The Lives of Shirley Graham Du Bois*, New York: New York University Press, 2000, pp. 212, and 252 - 253).

Shirley Graham Du Bois died in Beijing, China, on 27 March 1977, as a Tanzanian. She was was accorded a state funeral:

"It was Saturday of April 1977 in Beijing, China. The auditorium at the Paposhan Cemetery for Revolutionaries was full. The vice premier, Chen Yung-kuei, and the widow of former premier Zhou Enlai were among the dignitaries present. The Communist Party chairman, Hua Kuo-feng, sent a wreath to this 'memorial meeting,' as did the embassies of Tanzania, Ghana, and Zambia.

These leaders and ordinary citizens had come to mourn the passing of a woman, born an African American, who died in China as a citizen of Tanzania.

Shirley Graham Du Bois—the name that most knew her by—was eighty years old and had come to the Chinese capital for medical treatment....

China was also quite close to Graham Du Bois's eventual adopted home, Tanzania; according to one analyst, Dar es Salaam by the early 1970s 'had probably developed more extensive ties with that country than with any other non-African state'....

Many of her duties as an activist and a writer concerned her 'motherland,' Africa. At a time when many African Americans shunned the continent in embarrassment because of its underdevelopment, she was presenting an alternative vision....

She wrote biographies of leading African personalities, worked at the shoulder of Nkrumah when he was seeking to build a 'United States of Africa,' and became a citizen of Ghana, then Tanzania....

(She eventually settled in Dar es salaam, Tanzania, although) Nkrumah advised her, recommending that she stay away from Tanzania in her search for a post-coup home, for 'East Africa at the moment is filled up with American agents—CIA and so forth. I don't trust these 'guys'....

She encountered many...exiles in Dar es Salaam, a frequent port of call for her after 1966 (the year she left Ghana soon after Nkrumah was overthrown). She became quite friendly with the nation's leader, Julius Nyerere, whom she addressed as 'my dear Mwalimu' or teacher.....When she traveled to the southeast African republic, she would meet with him 'not only in his office, but with the family in his home.' Her affection for the Tanzanian leader was revealed in her hagiographic biography of him." – (Ibid., pp. 25, 27, 29, 217, and 251).

Her support for Nkrumah had cost her dearly. But Nkrumah remained a respected figure in the African-American community; his stature as a Pan-Africanist icon enhanced by the belief that it was the United States which was behind the military coup against him; a coup that was partly attributed to Nkrumah's bitter criticism of the United States in his book, *Neo-Colonialism: The Last Stage of Imperialism.* As Robert Smith, a former American ambassador to Ghana, stated in an interview:

"Nkrumah dropped the straw that broke the camel's back, so to speak, in that he published a new book called *Neo-Colonialism (The Last State of Imperialism)*...which was simply outrageous. It accused the United States of every sin imaginable to man. We were blamed for everything in the world.

The book was so bad that I remember the then Assistant Secretary (of state for African affairs), G. Mennen Williams, called me up and gave me that book and said, 'Bob, I know this is bad. I don't know how bad. I want you to take it home tonight and read it. You're not going to get any sleep and I apologize for that, but on my desk, by eight o'clock tomorrow morning, I've got to have a written summary of this because I have called the Ghanaian ambassador in at ten o'clock tomorrow morning. We're going to protest this book.'

There had already been advance publicity so we knew it was bad, but we hadn't had our hands on a copy. And it was everything we feared it would be. It was awful.

And the next morning – of course, he had me in on this meeting as the note taker – a lovely, old man, Michael Ribiero, was the Ghanaian ambassador. Hated Nkrumah privately, but was a good soldier trying to put the best face on this, a career officer in their foreign service and very respected here and in Ghana.

Governor Williams, of course, was a relatively mild-mannered man. I had never heard Soapy Williams raise his voice until that conversation. Neither have I ever heard an ambassador get a tongue lashing like Ribiero got from Assistant Secretary Williams that morning. He, unfortunately, tried a couple times to interrupt the governor when he was making a point. He had my notes in front of him. And at one point, when Ribiero interrupted him, he said, 'Just a minute, Mr. Ambassador, don't interrupt me. I'm not through.' And he continued to go on.

He was raising his voice. He was shaking his finger in the ambassador's face. And it was a very painful, hour-long interview. To put it mildly, he protested vigorously the contents and publication of this book.

I think the publication of that book might also have contributed in a material way to his overthrow shortly thereafter." – (Ambassador Robert P. Smith, interviewed by Charles Stuart Kennedy, 28 February 1989, *The Association for Diplomatic Studies and Training, Foreign Affairs Oral History Project*, pp. 12 – 15).

The book was Marxist in terms of analysis and Leninist in ideological orientation with regard to the imperialist nature of capitalism as a predatory system and imperialism being the highest stage of capitalism, thus in accord with Nkrumah's thinking although it was ghost-written. But it was Nkrumah who propounded the work's central thesis. Also, it was he who coined the term "neo-colonialism" to describe the insidious nature of the machinations of the imperial powers to dominate and control former colonies after they attained sovereign status.

The central thesis of *Neo-Colonialism: The Last Stage of Imperialism* also reflected Nkrumah's profound mistrust – perhaps even hatred – of the United States as an imperial power ruthlessly exploiting Africa and wreaking havoc across the continent; a belief that was reinforced by what happened during the Congo crisis, including Lumumba's assassination, for which the United States was largely responsible.

He gave a passionate speech at the United Nations, accusing imperial – Western – powers of interfering in African affairs in an attempt to control the destiny of the continent, and even wrote a book, *Challenge of the Congo: A Case Study of Foreign Pressures in an Independent State*, to explain what happened in "the bleeding heart of Africa" during that period and what needed to be done for African countries to be genuinely independent.

His memory is invoked even today whenever there is a crisis in Africa attributed to disunity among Africans and whenever there is foreign intervention in continental affairs to serve the interests of external forces; the lesson being: had African leaders agreed to unite their countries under one government as Nkrumah advocated, none of this would be happening. And although many of his arguments lacked originality, there is no question that he was very good at using Marxist arguments in different analytical contexts to justify his position.

He was also probably the most daring African leader in the continent's post-colonial history, demonstrated by his passionate call for immediate continental unification under one government and for the invasion of Rhodesia by Ghanaian troops to overthrow the white minority regime; goals most of his colleagues thought were unrealistic and even reckless as well as premature considering the fact that other African leaders were not ready to relinquish power for the sake of continental unity, and the invasion of Rhodesia by Ghanaian forces would have been a logistical nightmare without the direct involvement of Tanzania and Zambia.

May be he thought by using the Ghanaian army to try and free Rhodesia, other African countries would have been forced to send troops to the combat zone had Nyerere and Kaunda supported his mission to use Tanzania and Zambia as operational and rear bases; an unlikely prospect during that time. Also, apartheid South Africa would have entered the war to support the white minority regime in Rhodesia. But that was Nkrumah, the visionary.

Yet, some of his lofty ideals did not correspond to reality; his quest for immediate continental unification in the sixties being the most unrealistic.

He ignored the formidable opposition he faced from other African leaders who did not want to unite their countries under one government; most of them didn't. They were not even interested in forming an exploratory committee which could have helped chart the course towards unification. That is why Nyerere told Nkrumah "We are not going to have an African Napoleon" who is going to force other African leaders to unite their countries now – or even in the future - if they were not ready or if they did not want to do so. A regional approach towards unity – for example, by forming economic blocs even before considering regional federation under one government - seemed to be more acceptable to some of them. As Nyerere stated in his speech in Accra on the 40th anniversary of Ghana's independence in March 1997:

"Prior to independence of Tanganyika, I had been

advocating that East African countries should federate and then achieve independence as a single political unit. I had said publicly that I was willing to delay Tanganyika's independence in order to enable all three-mainland countries to achieve their independence together as a single federated state.

I made the suggestion because of my fear, proved correct by later events, that it would be very difficult to unite our countries if we let them achieve independence separately.

Once you multiply national anthems, national flags and national passports, seats at the United Nations, and individuals entitled to 21-gun salute, not to speak of a host of ministers, prime ministers, and envoys, you will have a whole army of powerful people with vested interests in keeping Africa balkanized. That was what Nkrumah encountered in 1965.

After the failure to establish the union government at the Accra summit of 1965, I heard one head of state express with relief that he was happy to be returning home to his country still head of state. To this day I cannot tell whether he was serious or joking. But he may well have been serious, because Kwame Nkrumah was very serious and the fear of a number of us to lose our precious status was quite palpable.

But I never believed that the 1965 Accra summit would have established a union government for Africa. When I say that we failed, that is not what I mean, for that clearly was an unrealistic objective for a single summit.

What I mean is that we did not even discuss a mechanism for pursuing the objective of a politically united Africa. We had a Liberation Committee already. We should have at least had a Unity Committee or undertaken to establish one. We did not. And after Kwame Nkrumah was removed from the African political scene nobody took up the challenge again."

One of Nyerere's critics and admirers, Professor Ali Mazrui, stated in some of his lectures and writings that it was Nyerere, not Nkrumah, who was vindicated by history on how African countries should pursue the goal of continental unity.

A few years before he died, Professor Mazrui also said "Nkrumah: The Leninist Czar" was the most controversial – and most influential – article he ever wrote and was still being debated in academic circles and elsewhere decades later.

He was strongly criticised by some of Nkrumah's supporters and admirers who denounced him as "an imperialist agent." Nkrumah himself, who read the article when he was in exile in Conakry, Guinea, said it was written by a black neo-colonial intellectual. The two first met in 1961 when Mazrui was a student at Columbia University in New York where he was studying for his master's degree in political science. Nkrumah spoke at Columbia during his visit to New York where he also addressed the United Nations. He also visited Harlem where he once lived when he was a student in the United States.

Mazrui angered even more Ghanaians when, in a lecture at the University of Ghana and elsewhere in Accra in the 2000s, and in some of his writings, he stated: "Nkrumah was a great African, but not a great Ghanaian." According to Mazrui himself:

"Most Ghanaian intellectuals seem aware of my notorious article of 1966 titled, 'Nkrumah: The Leninist Czar.' The article has two controversial arguments. Firstly, while Nkrumah was ideologically a Leninist, he was in style of governance a Czar when he was in power. An even more explosive paradox of mine was that Nkrumah was a great African, but not a great Ghanaian.

In 2007, as during my earlier visits to Ghana, I was repeatedly questioned about those two assertions. Militant

Nkrumahists and members of his old party (the C.P.P.) were outraged by my views and argued back vehemently both at my lectures and during radio phone-in interviews.

At another lecture I gave at the W.E.B. Du Bois Pan-African Cultural Centre in Accra the debate about Nkrumah exploded into a walkout by a couple of enraged Nkrumahists.

But we should remember that Ghana continues to be deeply divided about Kwame Nkrumah, their most illustrious post-colonial son and their founder president. There are at least as many Ghanaians who agree with my conclusions about Nkrumah as disagree." – (Ali A. Mazrui, *Mazrui Newsletter No. 32*, Spring 2008, p. 13).

It is a highly contentious subject, especially when one takes into account the fact that it was Nkrumah who laid the foundation for modern Ghana – the infrastructure, industrialisation, and so on. Yet the argument persists that "he was not a great Ghanaian" because he pursued his Pan-African goals at the expense of Ghana, including liberation and continental unification under one socialist government, probably a Marxist one since he was a Marxist himself; a position that was somewhat different from Nyerere's in terms of continental unity. As Nyerere stated in an interview with Ikaweba Bunting of the *New Internationalist*:

"For me liberation and unity were the most important things. I have always said that I was African first and socialist second. I would rather see a free and united Africa before a fragmented socialist Africa. I did not preach socialism. I made this distinction deliberately so as not to divide the country.

The majority in the anti-colonial struggle were nationalist. There was a minority who argued that class was the central issue, that white workers were exploited as black workers by capitalism. They wanted to approach liberation in purely Marxist terms. However, in South Africa white workers oppressed black workers. It was more than class and I saw that....

Even now for me freedom and unity are paramount." – (Mwalimu Julius K. Nyerere, in an interview with Ikaweba Bunting, *New Internationalist*, Oxford, UK, December 1998).

Unlike Nyerere, Nkrumah was a Marxist throughout his political career. In fact, he embraced Marxism in the early forties when he was a student in the United States. Years later, he even wrote a book, *Class Struggle in Africa*, based on Marxist analysis.

Colin Legum, in his review of Nkrumah's first book, *Towards Colonial Freedom*, also clearly stated that Nkrumah's political thought – at least a substantial part of it on social, political and economic theory - was a product of Marxism and Leninism. As he stated:

"*Towards Colonial Freedom* is a restatement of imperialism as propounded by Lenin. Dr. Nkrumah has, of course, never concealed his own Marxist beliefs." – (Colin Legum, *The Journal of Modern African Studies, Vol. 1, Issue 01*, March 1963, pp. 125 – 126).

Nkrumah's book, whose whole title was *Towards Colonial Freedom: Africa in the Struggle Against World Imperialism*, was first published in London in October 1947 when Nkrumah was not yet actively involved in politics in his home country, the Gold Coast. He returned to the Gold Coast – from the UK – on a ship with his friend and classmate at Lincoln University, Ako Adjei, in November 1947.

Ako Adjei himself played a major role in the struggle for Ghana's independence – he was one of The Big Six who led the anti-colonial struggle as members of the United Gold Coast Convention (UGCC) – but later fell out with Nkrumah and was imprisoned by him. In fact, it was he who recommended Nkrumah to the UGCC leaders to be the party's secretary-general, only to be imprisoned later by his erstwhile friend on false charges of treason after Nkrumah became president.

Besides Lenin, Nkrumah's book (*Towards Colonial Freedom*) and his analysis of imperialism was also based on the work of Rosa Luxemburg.

Nkrumah himself, in acknowledgement of his Marxist beliefs, embraced scientific socialism – developed by Marx and Engels – as the only form of true socialism, thus differing with Nyerere who espoused African socialism. As Ama Biney states in her book, *The Political and Social Thought of Kwame Nkrumah*:

"During the four years Nkrumah spent in Conakry, through his letters to various individuals, his thinking on many social, political, and economic issues can be delienated.

When his research assistant, June Milne, expressed an interest in writing a book on Nkrumaism, Nkrumah wrote, 'The most tantalising part of it will be my Marxist or socialist ideology. You know I am a Marxist and scientific socialist. But I don't consider myself in this particular sense a Leninist. Leninism is an application of Marxism to the Russian milieu. But the Russian milieu is not the same as the African milieu. And here the question of communism comes in – whether I am a communist or not. I am a scientific socialist and a Marxist and if that is tantamount to being a communist then I am. But not a communist of the Marxist-Leninist type.'

Here Nkrumah openly acknowledged his Marxist beliefs. He considered Marxism to be a nondogmatic tool applied to different social and economic conditions. However, he did not define what type of communist he was and, therefore, ambiguity remains as to his definition. In short, Nkrumah was undoctrinaire in his application of

Marxist analysis to African realities." – (Ama Biney, *The Political and Social Thought of Kwame Nkrumah*, New York: Palgrave Macmillan, 2011, pp. 162 – 163).

Sharply contrasted with that is Nyerere's position on Marxism-Leninism and scientific socialism. His position is rooted in indigenous thought, instead of embracing imported -isms such as Marxism to find solutions to African problems. He was not a doctrinaire socialist like those who espoused Marxist dogma. As he stated in his book, *Freedom and Socialism*:

"There is no theology of socialism. There is, however, an apparent tendency among certain socialists to try and establish a new religion – a religion of socialism itself. This is usually called 'scientific socialism' and the works of Marx and Lenin are regarded as the holy writ in the light of which all other thoughts and actions have to be judged....Its proponents are often most anxious to decry religion as the 'opium of the people,' and they present their beliefs as 'science.' Yet they talk and act in the same manner as the most rigid of theologians.

We find them condemning one another's actions because they do not accord with what the priests of 'scientific socialism' have decided is the true meaning, in modern terms, of books written more than 100 years ago.

Indeed we are fast getting to the stage where quarrels between different Christian sects about the precise meaning of the Bible fade into insignificance when compared with the quarrels of those who claim to be the true interpreters of Marxism-Leninism!

This attempt to create a new religion out of socialism is absurd. It is not scientific, and it is almost certainly not Marxist – for however combatant and quarrelsome a socialist Marx was, he never claimed to be an infallible divinity! Marx was a great thinker. He gave a brilliant analysis of the industrial capitalist society in which he lived; he diagnosed its ills and advocated certain remedies which he believed would lead to the development of a healthy society. But he was not God.

The years have proved him wrong in certain respects just as they have proved him right in others. Marx did not write revealed truth; his books are the result of hard thinking and hard work, not a revelation from God. It is therefore unscientific to appeal to his writings as Christians appeal to the Bible, or Muslims to the Koran.

The works of Marx and Lenin are useful to a socialist because these men thought about the objective conditions of their time and tried to work out the actions necessary to achieve certain ends. We can learn from their methods of analysis, and from their ideas. But the same is true of many other thinkers of the past.

It is no part of the job of a socialist in 1968 to worry about whether or not his actions or proposals are in accordance with what Marx or Lenin wrote, and it is a waste of time and energy to spend hours – if not months and years – trying to prove that what you have decided is objectively necessary is really in accordance with their teachings.

The task of a socialist is to think out for himself the best way of achieving desired ends under the conditions which exist now. It is his job to think how to organize society, how to solve a particular problem, or how to effect certain changes, in a manner which will emphasize the importance of man and the equality of man.

It is especially important that we in Africa should understand this. We are groping our way forward towards socialism, and we are in danger of being bemused by this new theology, and therefore of trying to solve our problems according to what the priests of Marxism say is what Marx said or meant. If we do this we shall fail.

Africa's conditions are very different from those of the Europe in which Marx and Lenin wrote and worked. To talk as if these thinkers provided all the answers to our problems, or as if Marx invented socialism, is to reject both the humanity of Africa and the universality of socialism. Marx did contribute a great deal to socialist thought. But socialism did not begin with him, nor can it end in constant reinterpretation of his writings.

Speaking generally, and despite the existence of a few feudalistic communities, traditional Tanzanian society had many socialist characteristics. The people did not call themselves socialists, and they were not socialists by deliberate design. But all the people were workers, there was no living off the sweat of others. There was no very great difference in the amount of goods available to the different members of the society. All these are socialist characteristics.

Despite the low level of material progress, traditional African society was in practice organized on a basis which was in accordance with socialist principles.

These conditions still prevail over large areas of Tanzania – and indeed in many other parts of Africa. Even in our urban areas, the social expectation of sharing what you have with your kinsfolk is still very strong – and causes great problems for individuals! These things have nothing to do with Marx; the people have never heard of him. Yet they provide a basis on which modern socialism can be built. To reject this base is to accept the idea that Africa has nothing to contribute to the march of mankind; it is to argue that the only way progress can be achieved in Africa is if we reject our own past and impose on ourselves the doctrines of some other society.

Nor would it be very scientific to reject Africa's past when trying to build socialism in Africa. For, scientific socialism means finding out all the facts in a particular situation, regardless of whether you like them or not, or whether they fit in with preconceived ideas. It means analysing these facts, and then working out solutions to the problems you are concerned with in the light of these facts, and of the objectives you are trying to achieve.

This is what Marx did in Europe in the middle of the nineteenth century; if he had lived in Sukumaland, Masailand, or Ruvuma, he would have written a different book than *Das Kapital*, but he could have been just as scientific and just as socialist. For if 'scientific socialism' means anything, it can only mean that the objectives are socialist and you apply scientific methods of study in working out the appropriate policies.

If the phrase does not mean that, then it is simply a trap to ensnare the unwary into a denunciation of their own nature therefore into a new form of oppression. For a scientist works to discover truth. He does not claim to know it, nor is he seeking to discover truth as revealed – which is the job of the theologian. A scientist works on the basis of the knowledge which has been accumulated empirically, and which is held to be true until new experience demonstrates otherwise, or demonstrates a superior truth which takes precedence in particular situations.

A really scientific socialist would therefore start his analysis of the problems of a particular society from the standpoint of that society. In Tanzania he would take the existence of some socialist values as part of his material for analysis; he would study the effect of the colonial era on these attitudes and on the systems of social organization; he would take account of the world situation as it affects Tanzania. After doing all that he would try to work out policies appropriate for the growth of a modern socialist state. And he could well finish up with the Arusha Declaration and the policies of ujamaa!

A scientific socialist could do all this with or without a knowledge and understanding of Marx and Lenin – or for that matter Saint-Simon, Owen or Laski. Knowledge of the work and thinking of these and other people may help a socialist to know what to look for and how to evaluate the things he sees; but it could also mislead him if he is not careful.

Equally, a knowledge of history may help him to learn from the experience of others; a knowledge of economics will help him to understand some of the forces at work in the society. But if he tries to use any of these disciplines and philosophies as a gospel according to which he must work out solutions he will go wrong. There is no substitute for his own hard work and hard thinking." – (Julius K. Nyerere, *Freedom and Socialism: A Selection from Writings and Speeches 1965 – 1967*, Dar es Salaam: Oxford University Press, 1968, pp. 14 – 17).

C.L.R. James hailed the Arusha Declaration, which Nyerere wrote in an attempt to transform Tanzania into a socialist society, as "the highest stage of resistance ever reached by revolting Blacks."

When Nyerere himself was asked in an interview in December 1998, "Does the Arusha Declaration still stand up today?", he said in response:

"I still travel around with it. I read it over and over to see what I would change. Maybe I would improve on the Kiswahili that was used but the Declaration is still valid: I would not change a thing.

Tanzania had been independent for a short time before we began to see a growing gap between the haves and the have-nots in our country. A privileged group was emerging from the political leaders and bureaucrats who had been poor under colonial rule but were now beginning to use their positions in the Party and the Government to enrich themselves. This kind of development would alienate the leadership from the people. So we articulated a new national objective: we stressed that development is about all our people and not just a small and privileged minority.

The Arusha Declaration was what made Tanzania distinctly Tanzania. We stated what we stood for, we laid down a code of conduct for our leaders and we made an effort to achieve our goals." – (Nyerere, and C.L.R. James, *New Internationalist*, ibid.)

C.L.R. James had this to say about Nyerere and Tanzania under Mwalimu's leadership:

"The opportunity arrived for me to go to Tanzania. I spent eight or ten days there. I talked to a lot of people, I travelled about a lot, I had an interview with Nyerere and I am satisfied that what they are doing is something entirely new, not only for Africa but in the political systems of the world that we have known. Nothing like it has appeared since Lenin died in 1924....

Nyerere has understood what has been the cause of the collapse of the other African states and knew that if he didn't put blocks in the road of that he was going to go the same way. This is the reason why this has taken place....

Nyerere...has introduced policies which strike at all the weaknesses of the colonial African state, all the weaknesses that have remained....Everything he says doesn't only come from a clever brain, but he is someone who is aware of what happened in Africa, in the African states, and knows that unless he takes the necessary steps it will happen to him....

Now the Arusha Declaration, Part V....Number One: 'Every TANU and Government leader must be either a Peasant or a Worker.'

Now that makes 15% of government people in every country absolutely excluded from the government. He does not want any business men in there at all. You must be either a peasant or a worker. And surely nobody associated with the practices of capitalism or feudalism. Now that could cause a revolution in 90% of the countries that exist in the world today.

Number Two: 'No TANU or Government leader should hold shares in any Company.' And if they propose that in the Caribbean, of course, there would be a revolution at once. In Britain and these other places, the ministers, when they are defeated in the political system, the Tories come in or the Labour Party comes in, when they go out they get shares and places in companies and so forth and they hold some of those places and receive money at times when they are actually members.

Nyerere has seen that sort of thing going on in African states and he says that is going to ruin us because it is a small section of the population that does this. So he says we don't want that at all.

He goes on to say 'No TANU or Government leader should hold Directorships in any privately owned enterprises.'

These are very drastic statements.

Now 'No TANU or Government leader should own houses which he rents to others.' That might seem an ordinary statement. What happens is this. This fellow becomes a Minister of the Government, or well established in the parliament or whatever they have and he goes to the bank and says 'I want to borrow ten or fifteen thousand pounds.' They give it to him. He goes to the local concrete people, and good carpenters, and so forth and he says 'I want to build a house.' And they build him a fine house. And he knows a lot of people who want housing, so he rents this house, and with the money he can pay back the bank. So he has a source of income there. Having built one, he goes out, borrows some more money builds another. So these fellows can have 4 or 5 houses and after five years they are drawing rents all the time.

That is what Nyerere is putting an end to. 'No TANU or Government leader should own houses which he rents to others.' That is not a general statement, it is a particular statement in that it is the way these fellows behave all over Africa and which makes the competition for government positions so terrific. Because you have the opportunity to do all these things.

Then point number six: 'For the purposes of this

Resolution, the term 'leader' should comprise the following (now look whom they call leaders): Members of the TANU National Executive Committee; Ministers, Members of Parliament, Senior Officials of Organizations affiliated to TANU,... all those appointed or elected under any clause of the TANU Constitution, councillors and Civil Servants in the high and middle cadres.'

In other words, anybody who is any kind of political leader in the government or in any kind of organization connected with the government is prohibited from taking part in all these things that ministers and their friends usually take part in. And in this context 'leader' means a man, a man and his wife; or a woman and her husband."

So the people there are no longer representatives of the old style of people who ruled, whether they are white, or black – they have cleared that up completely. That is the Arusha Declaration. It is not an article, it is not a speech, it is a statement of position by the government and that is what the people have to learn to do.

Now it isn't easy to manage. This is an extremely difficult thing, but all the young people and those in the universities, etc., are being brought up with this as government policy, and Nyerere really hopes that in time a new generation will come up which will govern itself by these objectives he has given to them, a new perspective, and the other African states had none but to carry on as best they could.

Now he talks about education and the new generation. Now, the great source of corruption in these governments is education, and the education you get, according to the European or American system, and then you join the government and all of you become a separate class.

And it really says quite clearly that one class of people in the state can exploit the other class. The people in the towns, the educated classes. Now, there are the few who go to secondary schools, are taken many miles away from their houses. They take you away to the secondary schools. You live in an enclave, You have to get their permission to go into the town for recreation but do not relate the work of town or country to your real life which is lived in the school compound. Later a few people go to the university.

If they are lucky enough to enter Dar-es-Salaam University College they live in comfortable quarters, eat well, and study hard for their degree. When they have been successful in obtaining it they know immediately that they will receive a salary of something like 660 pounds per annum. This is what they have been aiming for. It is what they have been encouraged to aim for.

They may also have the desire to serve the community but their idea of service is related to status and the salary which a university education is expected to confer upon its recipient. Those are the sources of the corruption of the African population and the African states. And Nyerere is determined to break that up. He says the salary and the status become a right automatically conferred by the degree.

You have to know the colonial situation to know the importance of this, because the large majority of the population are illiterate. And those who get the education s it in the seats of power and really control everything and are separate from the rest of the population. And they have so much power and there is so much to be got. That is why they fight so desperately for it. And that is why Nyerere has seen that he has to finish with that.

And then he goes on to say, 'It is wrong to criticize the young people for these attitudes. The new university graduate has spent the larger part of his life separated and apart from the masses of Tanzania.'

That is gospel truth. In the Caribbean it is the same. His parents may be poor but he has never fully shared that poverty. The moment you go into secondary education you are at once removed and you live a different life and your aim is at something that separates you from the population, which substantially is an illiterate backward population.

So, he says, his parents may be poor but he has never shared that poverty, he does not know what it is like to live as a poor peasant. He would be more at home in the world of the educated than he is among his own parents. Only during vacations has he spent time at home and even then he would often find that his parents and relatives support his own conception of his difference and regard it as wrong that he should live and work as the ordinary person that he really is.

In one or two novels they have singled out certain persons as characteristic of certain types, but a clear analytical statement of the situation in a colonial country – I have not seen it anywhere. This is what happens. In the Caribbean it is happening and in African territories it is worse because the population is illiterate and backward and they are being educated to hold important positions in the government and they become a special class. And as Nyerere says, 'They are exploiting the people.' And he wants to put an end to that.

He says, the third point is that our present system encourages the pupils in the idea that all knowledge which is worthwhile is acquired from books or from educated people. The knowledge and wisdom of old people is despised and they themselves regard it as being ignorant and of no account.' And he is trying to break up that situation.

The real source of corruption in these colonies is the secondary school and those who enter higher education, for they form automatically a section of society which can only exploit the mass of the population. They are in such a situation that in order to help they must get paid for it. And whether or not their own parents give them this impression of status, etc. That is what he is against.

This is why in regard to the secondary schools he says, 'Thus when this scheme is in operation, the secondary school has got to make its own money.' He says, 'They have to go and clear their own bush to build their own schools.' And when you hear as African say that they have to clear their own bush you know there is real bush in Africa. In Britain you have 15 or 20 elm trees, they put a fence round it and call it a forest. But Nyerere says, 'You have to clear your own bush, you have to plant, you have to make money, and don't expect any money from the government. The secondary school has got to make its own money, draw its profits and then decide what it is going to do.'

He says, 'Thus when this scheme is in operation, the revenue side of school accounts would not read as it does at present – grant from government., grant from voluntary agency or other charity. They would read – income from sale of cotton, value of the food grown and consumed, value of labour done by pupils on new building, repairs, equipment, etc. Government subvention, nil. Grant from government nothing.'

You would be startled if you were told that you were going to secondary school and you have to go out and make some money and determine how the school will go by the amount of money you made. I have not read this anywhere.

Rousseau is the man who has made the conception of the modern individual, but nowhere have I read in any place at all that the secondary school must become a school in which people make their own money and learn the kind of work and activity which is carried on by the mass of population.

Otherwise, they will certainly be separated from them and will not be able to teach them what is required, because they are going to live an agricultural life for as far as they could see and these students must not learn what is required by the professional classes and must not learn what separates them from the rest of the population, the very education that they practise, the schools that they make: What they do in the schools must prepare them to educate the mass of the population. Otherwise this separation will take place and the whole thing will fall apart.

I think that the most important thing that I can't tell you about Nyerere is this. On the slopes of the Cavarando there *are* some African families who have done pretty well. They have done what the British and the Americans and the Germans taught them – you have a piece of land, you have to work at it, you have to sell, you have to save your money up, then you employ some labour. And these fellows are very successful, the land is good, there is a lot of water and they have done extremely well. And what Nyerere says is that those people, we can't be hard on them, but we don't want the rest of the population to do what they have done because everybody told them, 'That is what is required.' And they are now employing some labour, making some money, spreading their good, becoming more and more expansive in regard to the land, etc. He says, we don't want that.

He says, what we have to aim at is the extension and development of the old African family because the African lived in the old days, and to some extent and in many places still lives, an extended, cooperative form of life. He says that is what we have to do. If we follow the habits of the people in western Europe and so forth and try to build up that we will wreck this country and we will never be able to put it in any kind of order. And it is very important to know that two of the greatest politicians of the 20th century had the same idea.

Gandhi mobilized the peasant and if he had not been able to mobilize the peasant the British would have been in India up to today. It was the mobilization of the peasant, those millions of people who have been removed from politics for so many centuries, that was the greatest shock. The British couldn't hold them in order. There were too many people involved.

And then Gandhi used to say, 'We have to take the peasant for what he is.' The peasant wears just a little shirt or something – Gandhi wore one! The peasant did not like any of them to deal with cows, but they got milk from the goat – Gandhi kept his goat and he milked the goat. The peasant wove the cloth he wore – Gandhi wove his own cloth. And he made it clear to everybody, and the peasant included, that their way of life was to be the foundation of the way of life.

He made it absolutely clear, he said 'Don't attempt to make these Indian peasants into peasants as in the advanced countries, as in Europe, etc. Number one, you can't do it, and in any case, take them for what they are.'

A second man who had very clear ideas about the peasant was Lenin. Lenin believed that the Russian peasant could only be changed if the Russian economy was assisted by the economy of the advanced countries who had become socialistic, because otherwise they *are* what they *are* and *we* can't leave them. So the two of them, different types of men were very clear as to what was to be done with the peasants. And I could show you how close Nyerere is to Lenin's proposal. Now, that is the situation. That is what he is doing.

He has not only nationalized, he has changed the political system completely, the social construction of people who are going to administer and take charge. He has made that into something new and altogether he is breaking up the aid system, the system which they have inherited, and which black people are trying to run and which is causing nothing but complete failure. Now I knew these fellows, I knew their limitations.

Fanon is much more severe, he made it perfectly clear that nothing could be settled in those African states unless the revolution was continued not only against the imperialists but against those who are going to succeed. That is what his book says. He says the revolution must go on. You cannot go on in this way and that is what Nyerere is doing. He is creating the elements of a new society. Some people complain to me and say, 'Don't you prefer that it should come from below?' I say, 'Sure it would be better if it would come from below, but it has come, and we should take it as it is.'

They have difficulties, sure they have difficulties but he has done splendidly. And Kaunda had followed him and I will read Kaunda:

'Now during the hazardous road to political independence we recognized the fact that Africa was going to be one of the biggest, if not the biggest battleground, for this century's ideological battle. As is well know, the present day ideological differences are based on certain economic and political theories and practices. Putting it very simply, one would say, it was a question of who owned or controlled the means of creating and distributing the wealth in any given nation.'

This is a key point, now follow what he is saying. For if the distribution of wealth is not done properly, it might lead to the creation of classes in society and the much valued humanist approach that is traditional and inherent in our African society would have suffered a final blow.

What he is saying is what Nyerere has been saying, the old African cooperative family structure is what we have to develop. We must not develop into some peasants who have done well and some who have not, or the whole structure is going to fall apart. It is very strange that very rapidly these African politicians, have seen it, they have to build on what is African. They have to build on the basic structure that these people have had for thousands of years.

They cannot try to develop a peasant on the economic structure of western civilization. That is sure to cause trouble and they cannot do it properly. This is something new that has appeared and I found in Africa that people are watching them. And I was told by many people, 'We don't know whether Nyerere will succeed, but if Nyerere is successful, the other African states will follow because they don't know where they are going, they are drifting along and if this is successful, they will go with it'....

They are trying to prevent a society building up the type of relation that exists in the advanced countries. They are not aiming at repetition of western society, they are hoping to build on the African basis and on what they have. Politically they would be creating room for opposing parties based on the oppressed and the oppressor concept which again would not be in keeping with the society described above....

Nyerere and TANU are beginning to find out, to restore, the African family, and to understand that this special group of people who are educated, who become bureaucrats, they are the ones who must be separated, they must be educated so as to become part of the population and bring the knowledge that they have as part of the population which the majority of the people constitute....Nothing like that has ever taken place in Africa anywhere.

Nkrumah, it seemed at the beginning, hoped to do something of the kind, but he didn't make these drastic changes in the economic and social structure that Nyerere has made, and it is my belief, I have talked to Nyerere, that he did it because he realized that unless these fundamental changes were made and the old structures and the ideas that the British and the French had left behind, unless these were completely cleared out and the people given another perspective, the degeneration of the African state was bound to continue....

Nyerere has realized that the government that he has is the same old imperialist colonial government and he is seeking to break it up. And he realizes that they cannot run it as well as the imperialists did. That is the situation. And the second point of Lenin's. Last time, I gave you fifty guesses, this time I give you a thousand. Lenin says, we have the peasants, the worst thing is to change that government, and the second thing is to conduct educational work among the peasants. When I showed it to Nyerere he said he hadn't read it anywhere. But I could recognize what he was going.

There are all sorts of passages which show that Lenin was aware of what was necessary, they had to break up that system and it is a very difficult thing to break up an old system. And if you try to run it you can't run it as well as the people who made it, who made it for themselves and knew what they were doing. And they are trying in African state, after African state to have black African people run what is essentially the old system with the worst economic possibilities. That is why they are in the mess they are in and that is why we must understand the seriousness and the radical approach which Nyerere has shown ...

Now my last word here is my African friend with his African socialism. African socialism must be flexible, it must make progress toward its main objectives. What Nyerere says is that African socialism must break up all the remnants of the system that we have inherited and institute something new. And then this young man goes on to say, 'Valid as Marx's description was, it bears little similarity to Kenya today.' On colonialism and so forth, they make it very clear that Marxism is something that Marx had to say about the advanced countries, it had no relation whatever to the colonial territories now that they have become independent.

The only relation they had to Marxism was to call themselves Socialism. But I was able to show that Nyerere has, in discovering the necessity of breaking up this system which he has inherited from the old imperialists, has discovered the same thing that Lenin after six years was telling the Russians....

There is one of the most important features of political

development in the world today, not only for the underdeveloped countries but, I am positive, I have examined it, the advanced countries, in their systems of education in particular, have a lot to learn from what is taking place in Tanzania." – (C.L.R. James, "Reflections on Pan-Africanism," ibid.)

Nyerere did a lot for Tanzania. He did his best to make sure that all the people, including the poorest and those who were illiterate, participated in the development of their country and had equal rights and access to the nation's resources without fear of being oppressed and exploited by the privileged few. The country and all its resources belonged to all Tanzanians.

Nkrumah also did a lot for Ghana in the few years he was in power. But he did not do enough to radically transform Ghana into a socialist society the way Nyerere did in Tanzania.

Still, like Nyerere, Nkrumah left a legacy, especially with regard to the continent's destiny, that is still being debated: Where would Africa be today had the continent united under one government in 1963 or soon thereafter, as he strongly advocated? Was it a realistic goal? Or was a regional approach to continental unification a more viable option? Would socialism have been adopted on a continental scale had African countries succeeded in uniting under one government? As Nyerere stated:

"Kwame Nkrumah and I were committed to the idea of unity. African leaders and heads of state did not take Kwame seriously. However, I did. I did not believe in these small little nations. Still today I do not believe in them. I tell our people to look at the European Union, at these people who ruled us who are now uniting.

Kwame and I met in 1963 and discussed African Unity. We differed on how to achieve a United States of Africa. But we both agreed on a United States of Africa as necessary. Kwame went to Lincoln University, a black college in the US. He perceived things from the perspective of US history, where 13 colonies that revolted against the British formed a union. That is what he thought the OAU (Organisation of African Unity) should do.

I tried to get East Africa to unite before independence. When we failed in this way, I was wary about Kwame's continental approach. We corresponded profusely on this. Kwame said my idea of 'regionalization' was only balkanization on a larger scale. Later, African historians will have to study our correspondence on this issue of uniting Africa." – (Nyerere, *New Internationalist*, ibid.)

Yet Nkrumah himself formed a regional federation – of Ghana, Guinea and Mali (with Guinea in 1958, and Mali joining in 1961) – but it collapsed; in fact, it was more symbolic than functional.

It was only after he failed in his attempt to form a functional union of the three West African countries that he started opposing regional federations, claiming they were no more than balkanisation of the continent on a grand scale. Even when he was in London for two and a half years, after he left the United States in May 1945, he worked with other West Africans in the UK in an attempt to form a West African federation in the future.

He did not see all that as balkanisation of Africa on a larger scale – until Nyerere tried to form a federation in East Africa and seemed to be succeeding in pursuit of that goal. Nkrumah did not like that. He wanted to be the first, but failed in his regional attempt to form a federation in West Africa.

He was resolutely opposed to formation of an East African federation and did everything he could to sabotage it. This infuriated Nyerere who, in pointed reference to Nkrumah, publicly stated at a press conference in Nairobi in June 1963 after the three East African leaders – Kenyatta, Obote and Nyerere himself – met to discuss forming a federation:

"We must reject some of the pretensions that have been made from outside East Africa. We have already heard the curious argument that the continued 'balkanisation' of East Africa will somehow help African unity.... These are attempts to rationalize absurdity." – (Julius Nyerere, quoted by Richard Cox, *Pan-Africanism in Practice: An East African Study*, Oxford University Press, 1964, p. 77; A. Mazrui, *Towards a Pax Africana*, op. cit., p. 71).

Nkrumah's interference in East African affairs angered Nyerere so much that he even wrote Nkrumah about it:

"His meddling became so apparent that on 6th August, 1963, President Nyerere of Tanzania wrote him a very angry letter on this subject." – Donald S. Rothchild, *Politics of Integration: An East African Documentary*, Institute of Development Studies, University College of Nairobi; East African Publishing House, Nairobi, Kenya, 1968, p. 112).

Nkrumah's interference in East Africa to frustrate and neutralise Nyerere's attempt to form an East African federation was one of the biggest mistakes of his political career and demonstrated that he was determined to undermine other African leaders who did not agree with him. As Basil Davidson stated in his book, *Black Star: A View of the Life and Times of Kwame Nkrumah*:

"Some, like Julius Nyerere of Tanzania, chastised Nkrumah for his interference. East Africa, Nyerere believed, could best contribute to continental unity by moving first towards regional unity.
Although knowing little about East Africa, Nkrumah not only disagreed but actively interfered to obstruct the

East African federation proposed by Nyerere.... It was one of Nkrumah's worst mistakes." – (Basil Davidson, *Black Star: A View of the Life and Times of Kwame Nkrumah*, Allen Lane, London, 1973, quoted by Geoffrey Mmari, "The Legacy of Nyerere," in Colin Legum and Geoffrey Mmari, eds., *Mwalimu: The Influence of Nyerere*, Africa World Press, Trenton, New Jersey, 1995, pp. 179 – 180).

Renowned Kenyan socio-political analyst, Philip Ochieng, who once worked as a columnist of the *Daily News*, Dar es Salaam, Tanzania, in the early seventies, stated in his article,"Did Nkrumah Kill Off the First EA Community?," in *The East African*, Nairobi, 28 March 2009:

"According to the story that I kept hearing...from top-level academics...at the University of Dar es Salaam... known to enjoy direct links with Mwalimu's State House, it was because Dr Nkrumah wanted to be the father figure of all the regional initiatives, that he sabotaged the East African chapter....

Nkrumah himself sponsored a West African initiative similar to the proposed East African federation...composed of his Ghana, Ahmed Sekou Toure's Guinea and Modibo Keita's Mali....As long as he was the paramount leader of such an initiative, there was no problem.

In East Africa, Nyerere was also taking serious steps to restructure his society. Tanzania (under Nyerere), indeed, is the African country that has gone farthest in dismantling the political, economic and intellectual pillars of colonialism....

Nkrumah...wanted to be the dominant figure in every regional initiative. Like Joseph Stalin for all of the world's non-Maoist communist parties, Nkrumah wanted to be chief policy-maker and policy implementer for every one of the regional groupings. The probable idea was that, if all those regional groupings decided to unite into a single continental government, no individual would be in a position to vie with the Ghanaian leader to be its first president.

That was why Nkrumah could not trust Mwalimu Nyerere as the intellectual spirit behind the East African proposal. For, although they seemed like ideological comrades, the old Tanganyikan schoolteacher was completely independent-minded and would never have been prepared to act as Nkrumah's regional poodle.

With Nyerere thus dismissed and Mzee Kenyatta accused of having surrendered Kenya as a backyard of corporate Britain, the Ubungo intellectuals explained that, in Nkrumah's eyes, Obote now appeared as the only one not too committed one way or the other. That was why – according to the story – it was Obote that Nkrumah latched onto to frustrate all the plans to federate."

Unfortunately for Nkrumah, he failed where his rival, Nyerere, succeeded. He formed the Ghana-Guinea Union which Mali later joined to form the Ghana-Guinea-Mali Union. It collapsed. It was a union only on paper.

By remarkable contrast, Nyerere succeeded in uniting Tanganyika with Zanzibar to form Tanzania. Nyerere also was on the way to forming an East African federation which Nkrumah strongly opposed. Nkrumah played a significant role in blocking formation of an East African federation which Nyerere would probably have presided over in the following years. He did his best to make sure Nyerere did not succeed in his venture. But he did not stop there.

He took his crusade against Nyerere to the OAU summit in Cairo in July 1964 where he hoped to mobilise support for his attempt to portray Nyerere as someone who was an obstacle to continental unity under one government because he wanted to form an East African federation which would only be balkanisation of Africa on a grand scale.

He also wanted to portray Nyerere as someone who

was not qualified to host and help train freedom fighters from the countries, especially those in southern Africa, which were still under white minority rule. Tanganyika had been chosen by other African leaders to be the headquarters of the OAU Liberation Committee when they first met in Addis Ababa, Ethiopia, to form the Organisation of African Unity. Nkrumah did not like that.

At the OAU summit in Cairo, Nyerere responded to Nkrumah's criticism and attacks by saying "Some people insist on African unity now, not because they care at all, but because they hope that some stupid historian in the future" will praise them for being the first to seek continental unity when others did not, thus getting satisfaction from being glorified as true Pan-Africanists; it was all for personal glory.

Professor Willard Scott Thompson, a renowned American scholar – John F. Kennedy once said Thompson would be president of the United States someday – provided a different version of what happened. He contended that Nyerere misunderstood Nkrumah. He stated that when Nkrumah said "an imperialist agent," he was not talking about Nyerere; he was talking about Congo-Leopoldville, a country in turmoil during that period because of foreign intervention, where it had once been suggested freedom fighters should be trained. As he stated in his book, *Ghana's Foreign Policy, 1957 – 1966: Diplomacy Ideology, and the new State*:

"In Cairo, when Nkrumah had persisted in raising the issue of union government through back door and side door, despite continual defeat, Senghor had commented: 'I think we have already pronounced ourselves on the fact that we cannot, at present, form a Pan-African government'....

Botsio (Ghana's minister of foreign affairs Kojo Botsio) arrived in Cairo in mid-July for the foreign ministers' meeting, with inflexible instructions (from

68

Nkrumah) to press for union government and a high command....

After Nkrumah's attacks on the proposed East African federation and what Nyerere thought was an accusation that Tanganyika was an imperialist agent, he decided that enough damage had been done. In the sessions remaining before his own speech he was seen writing, obviously recasting his speech.

According to Botsio, Nkrumah's own speech had been reconstructed in part at the last minute; thus several references in it were ambiguous. As one result, Nyerere misread Nkrumah's attack on the (OAU) liberation committee (based in Dar es Salaam). Nyerere was right in saying that the only reason Ghana had criticized the committee was that the Addis Ababa conference 'had committed the unforgivable crime of not including Ghana on the Committee.' Nkrumah – and Nyerere quoted – had said:

'The choice of the Congo as a training base for freedom fighters was a logical one and there was every reason to accept the offer of the Congolese Government to provide offices and accommodation for the representatives of the Liberation *Committee* [i.e. Movements]. Africa's freedom fighters should not, however, have been exposed to the espionage, intrigues, frustrations and disappointments which they have experienced in the last 8 months. What would be the result of entrusting the training of freedom fighters against imperialism into the hands of an imperialist agent?'

Nyerere incorrectly concluded that Nkrumah believed that the headquarters of the liberation *committee* should have been in Léopoldville, and had instead been located in Dar-es-Salaam, a place of 'espionage and intrigue' (with freedom fighters trained, at that, by an 'imperialist agent). Nkrumah had referred only to the Congo in this section of his speech, and had meant to say 'Liberation *Movements,*' as indicated in the quoted passage.

His mistake made Nyerere's misunderstanding natural, although Nyerere's reading of it is contradicted on internal evidence. Yet there was enough in Nkrumah's speech that Nyerere did get right to make this confusion almost negligible; certainly most African governments at the time were not interested in the clarification....

The official version of Nkrumah's speech, 'The Quest for a United Africa,' Accra, 1964 (printed after the conference), uses the word 'MOVEMENTS' at a the crucial passage. There is no question that Nkrumah meant 'movements,' by all accounts. Nkrumah obviously knew the 'committee' was headquartered in Dar....

According to Botsio, Nyerere later apologized for the misunderstanding, but according to Tanzanian sources, the apology was only directed to the specific point, not to the substance of the speech." – (Willard Scott Thompson, *Ghana's Foreign Policy, 1957 – 1966: Diplomacy Ideology, and the new State,* Princeton, New Jersey, USA: Princeton University Press, 1969, pp. 350, 352, 353. See also Nkrumah's speech in Cairo in July 1964 when he criticised the OAU Liberation Committee and when he talked about "an imperialist agent," quoted in BBC, IV, No. 1611, 22 July 1964, cited by W.S. Thompson, ibid., p. 352).

By that time, when the African leaders met in Cairo in July 1964, Nyerere had already been entrusted with the training of the freedom fighters the previous year when the OAU chose Tanzania to be the headquarters of the OAU Liberation Committee.

Therefore, it is easy to understand why Nkrumah seemed to be talking about Nyerere, and not a Congolese leader in Leopoldville, when he said Africa should not trust "an imperialist agent" to be in charge of the training of the freedom fighters. It seemed he was not talking about

President Joseph Kasavubu. May be he was talking about Moise Tshombe who was prime minister of Congo-Leopoldville under Kasavubu during that time when he gave his speech at the OAU summit in Cairo, talking about "an imperialist agent"; which Tshombe was. Nkrumah himself had earlier, on 12 August 1960, written Tshombe about Tshombe's collaboration with the imperialists in destroying Congo. As he stated in the letter:

"You have assembled in your support the foremost advocates of imperialism and colonialism in Africa and the most determined opponents of African freedom. How can you, as an African, do this?" – (Nkrumah, in his letter to Moise Tshombe, 12 August 1960, reproduced in Ghana Government's White Paper, No. 6/60, p. 8, Accra, Ghana, August 1960; and in A. Mazrui, *Towards a Pax Africana*, op. cit., p. 38).

Nyerere also called Tshombe a traitor. As he stated in his address to the National Assembly of the United Arab Republic in Cairo on 9 April 1967:

"It is not possible for African states to compromise on the basic principles of African freedom and African equality. A leader like Tshombe, who was willing to employ South African racialists in order to maintain his own power, and who was willing to dismember an African state if he could not control it – such a man could obviously not bring his nation into a coherent African entity. But the reason is not that his economic policies involved compromise with the exploiters of Africa. The reason is his deliberate betrayal of the basic principles of African freedom and African equality. To negotiate with such a man would be equivalent to negotiating with the present regime in South Africa." – (Nyerere, "A New Look at Conditions for Unity," *Freedom and Socialism*, op. cit., pp. 295 – 296).

71

Other observers such as Ali Mazrui, unlike Professor Thompson, reached the same conclusion Nyerere did – that when Nkrumah talked about "an imperialist agent" being entrusted with the training of the freedom fighters, he was talking about Nyerere since the freedom fighters were based in Tanzania, not in Congo.

And the fact that Nkrumah changed parts of his speech at the last minute, resulting in several ambiguous references in the text, seems to suggest that the ambiguity was deliberate, intended to cause some confusion and cast doubt on Nyerere as a true Pan-Africanist and portray him as "an imperialist agent" despite all the evidence to the contrary, especially when Tanzania had already been chosen to be the headquarters of all the African liberation movements.

Also, there was a major difference between the two leaders – Nkrumah and Nyerere – in the way they pursued continental unity, which was partly fuelled by their adversarial relationship although they also worked together on a number of major issues more than they did with other African leaders with the exception of Nasser, Ben Bella, Sekou Toure and Modibo Keita who were also their ideological compatriots and close friends – members of a secret group within the OAU known as "The Group of Six," according to what Ben Bella said in an interview in Geneva, Switzerland, in 1995.

Unlike most African leaders, Nkrumah wanted immediate continental unification; Nyerere preferred the regional approach and said several times – before, during, and after the Cairo summit – that he agreed with Nkrumah on the need for a continental government but it could not be established immediately. In fact, he was one of the very few leaders – together with Nkrumah, Sekou Toure, Modibo Keita and Sourou-Migan Apithy – who strongly believed African countries should unite under one government.

Also, Nkrumah did not want the OAU Liberation Committee to be based in the country of his rival – although his ideological compatriot as well – Nyerere; hence his scathing criticism of both Nyerere and the Committee. As Professor William Burnett Harvey stated in his book, *Law and Social Change in Ghana*:

"The signing of the O.A.U. Charter abated the sharpness of the Casablanca-Monrovia split without removing the underlying causes. The continuing divisions were dramatically illustrated by the acid exchange between Dr. Nkrumah and President Nyerere of Tanganyika and Zanzibar at the Heads of State meeting in Cairo in July, 1964. The clash was precipitated by an address by Dr. Nkrumah urging immediate establishment of a United Government of Africa; in this speech he attacked the performance of the Liberation Committee established at Addis Ababa to assist the 'Freedom Fighters' in the still-dependent territories.

According to Dr. Nkrumah, the Freedom Fighters had been exposed to 'espionage, intrigues, frustrations and disappointments,' had been denied food, clothing and medicine and proper facilities for training. He complained that the Congo (Leopoldville) rather than Tanganyika was the 'logical' training base for Freedom Fighters. In a curious rhetorical question he asked, 'What could be the result of entrusting the training of Freedom Fighters against imperialism into the hands of an imperialist agent?' For all these ills, Nkrumah found the cure in the immediate establishment of a United Government of Africa.

Dr. Nyerere responded with understandable heat. He pointed out that Ghana was the only country that had made no financial contribution to the work of the Liberation Committee; he insisted that Ghana's failure to contribute had not resulted from the inadequate performance of the Committee but that the decision had in fact been made at

Addis Ababa when Ghana was not given membership on the Committee and Dar es Salaam had been chosen as the Committee's headquarters.

Dr. Nyerere declared that he was becoming increasingly convinced that the African states were divided 'between those who genuinely want a Continental Government and will work patiently for its realization; and those who simply use a phrase 'Union Government,' for the purposes of propaganda.' Clearly in his judgment, Ghana fell into the latter category.

Dr. Nyerere did 'not believe that there is a choice between achieving African unity step by step and achieving it in one act. The one-act choice is not available to us except in some curious imagination.'" – (William Burnett Harvey, *Law and Social Change in Ghana*, Princeton, New Jersey, USA: Princeton University Press, 1966, p. 169).

Also, Nkrumah's determination to block formation of an East African federation not only tarnished his image; it enhanced Nyerere's credentials as a realist in the quest for continental unity. As Nyerere put it: "When you set out to build a house, you don't begin by putting on the roof; first you start by laying the foundations." And according to Professor Mazrui:

"Nyerere...denounced Nkrumah's attempt to deflate the East African federation movement as petty mischief-making arising from Nkrumah's own sense of frustration in his own Pan-African ventures....He went public with his attack on Nkrumah. He referred to people who pretended that they were in favour of African continental union when all they cared about was to ensure that 'some stupid historian in the future' praised them for being in favour of the big continental ambition before anyone else was willing to undertake it....

On balance, history has proved Nkrumah wrong on the

74

question of Nyerere's commitment to liberation. Nyerere was second to none in that commitment.

At that Cairo conference of 1964 Nkrumah had asked 'What could be the result of entrusting the training of Freedom Fighters against imperialism into the hands of an imperialist agent?'

In the debates between incremental Pan-Africanism and rapid unification Nkrumah found a rival in Julius K. Nyerere of Tanzania....Nkrumah and Nyerere had already begun to be rivals as symbols of African radicalism before the coup which overthrew Nkrumah. Nkrumah was beginning to be suspicious of Nyerere in this regard....The two most important issues over which Nyerere and Nkrumah before 1966 might have been regarded as rivals for continental pre-eminence were the issues of African liberation and African unity." – (Ali A. Mazrui in his lecture "Nkrumahism and The Triple Heritage: Out of the Shadows" at the University of Ghana-Legon in 2002. See also Nyerere, "When you set out to build a house,..." at the OAU summit, Cairo, Egypt, July 1964, quoted by Colin Legum, "The Goal of an Egalitarian Society," in Colin Legum and Geoffrey Mmari, eds., *Mwalimu: The Influence of Nyerere*, op. cit., p. 191).

Professor Mazrui's version that Nkrumah did, indeed, call Nyerere "an imperialist agent" (out of frustration with Nyerere's rise and influence as a continental leader, threatening to eclipse Nkrumah is some respects, after Tanzania was chosen by other African leaders to be the headquarters of the OAU Liberation Committee) also seems to be consistent with the sequence of events before and after the Cairo summit in July 1964 when the two African leaders clashed.

It is also possible Nyerere misunderstood Nkrumah, and that Nkrumah was referring to somebody else in Congo-Leopoldville – probably Prime Minister Moise Tshombe – when he said "an imperialist agent."

But whatever Nkrumah said and meant in the larger context of his speech in Cairo was still consistent with his own image as Africa's leader. He saw himself as Africa's pre-eminent leader who did not want to be challenged or surpassed by anybody, demonstrated by his determination to undermine Nyerere's attempt to form an East African federation whose success would have earned Nyerere the distinction of being the first champion of regional integration to achieve his goal of helping unite countries under one government. Nkrumah did not want Nyerere to succeed and be surpassed by him in the quest for unity even on a regional scale, while Nkrumah himself had failed to achieve the same goal in West Africa.

A highly influential Nigerian newspaper, the *West African Pilot* founded by Dr. Nnamdi Azikiwe in 1937 (and edited by him from 1937 to 1947) even challenged Nkrumah and Nasser for considering themselves to be *the* continental leaders; a point underscored in the paper's editorial in May 1961:

"Until recently it was a tournament between Nasser and Nkrumah but Africa today contains many stars and meteorites, all of them seeking positions of eminence." – (*West African Pilot*, 18 May 1961; see also *West Africa*, London, 6 May 1961, quoted by A. Mazrui, *Towards a Pax Africana*, op. cit., p. 66).

Nkrumah was virtually isolated at the summit in Cairo besides the support he got from Sekou Toure, Modibo Keita, and Sourou-Migan Apithy of Dahomey in his quest for immediate continental unification. But even they, may be with the exception of President Apithy, did not go far enough to satisfy him. The collapse of the Ghana-Guinea-Mali Union, a pet creature of Nkrumah, demonstrated that even the three ideological compatriots – Nkrumah, Toure and Keita – could not work together to transform their union into a functional entity; it was virtually stillborn.

The adversarial relationship between Nkrumah and Nyerere, with regard to liberation and continental unity, was further addressed by Professor Thompson, as was Nkrumah's failure to convince his colleagues to agree to form one continental government:

"What Nyerere stopped by his speech was the politeness about union government. Tanganyika had, as he pointed out, practiced unity by uniting with Zanzibar; less 'preaching' about unity was needed.

He mocked union government as the panacea for every difficulty that Africa encountered, and also added his own invective: 'to cap this whole series of absurdities, after all the wonderful arguments against unity in East Africa, we are now told again, at this very rostrum, that those who are ready should go ahead and unite (as Nkrumah said in his speech). Those who are ready should now go ahead and unite. Now we have the permission to go ahead....If I were a cynic, I would say we of the United Republic of Tanganyika and Zanzibar are ready. I would ask Ghana to join our United Republic. But I am not a cynic.'

Nyerere's suggestion was no less logically compelling than any of the long line of Nkrumah's proposals, and now they were publicly declared to be nonsense. Nyerere had merely said the Emperor wore no clothes....

The speech was also significant as an opening of the sluice-gate for anti-Ghana feelings on many issues throughout Africa, and it signaled the beginning of the last stage of an 'anti-Nkrumah offensive' that was gaining support across the continent.

Nkrumah had been severely humiliated among his peers. Nonetheless,...the (OAU) decided to hold its second conference of heads of state in Accra, as the Ghanaians had suggested....Nkrumah insisted on bringing up union government.

Sékou Touré, the chairman, noted that the committee named at the foreign ministers' session had only asked the heads of state 'to declare itself on principle.' But Nkrumah insisted on pleading his case, and it is interesting to see what he said amidst his peers:

'What I am suggesting...I didn't say we should set out on this table and within five minutes establish a Union Government....My point was this, that it is a central factor in the political life of the African continent, since it is going to be a vital issue let us at least accept in principle the possibility of the establishment of a Union Government of Africa....But I say let's say that we should start here and then, and get all the functions and I put forward the suggestion also that we have been able to agree in principle to the possibility of the establishment of Union Government in Africa.

I say let's submit it to the...Jurist's Committee...so...what I am saying is...if it is a good idea then what I put forward is this: Let us give a chance to our Jurist's Committee....But I want to make it clear. I didn't come here to say---I know Rome wasn't built in a day but Rome started somewhere before it became Rome.'

Touré, as chairman – and Nkrumah's ally – tried to summarize the argument as logically as possible and Keita even added that the gap that 'had separated our friend...from the majority...was narrowing.' Apithy of Dahomey evoked memories of Nkrumah's 1947 London pan-African gathering which he had attended, and supported Nkrumah, by this time a picture of pathos.

Sir Abubakar (Tafawa Balewa) let them go no further. An African government was a dream, he said, 'Or a nightmare.' Nigeria, for its part, would never surrender its sovereignty. 'This request, Mr. Chairman, is indirectly a vote of no confidence in the Organisation of African Unity. When we started this Organisation only a year ago we were working, progressing and now we are trying to impose something.' Union government might come, so might world government, he said.

The Emperor of Ethiopia, who knew that at this point it was conceding nothing to grant Nkrumah some concession, and who possessed a sense of dignity, sought to blur the distinctions Sir Abubakar and others were making. 'The proposal of His Majesty [said the interpreter] is to examine the draft, not to reject it.' But Cameroun did not want to examine something that could not be implemented 'before five, ten, fifteen, or even twenty years,' and Bourguiba suggested that the appointment of such a committee would reduce the credibility of the OAU." – (Ibid., pp. 353, and 355).

Nkrumah somewhat saw the absurdity of his quest for immediate continental unification and the impractical nature of his proposal, as was clearly demonstrated by the overwhelming opposition he faced at the OAU summits in Cairo in July 1964 and even in his own capital Accra in October 1965. But he never gave up in spite of the fact that he was virtually isolated at both conferences:

"With almost any issue of concern to the radical African nationalists, Nkrumah might have taken the lead and increased his influence; he did do this with the Rhodesian question. The question of continental union government, however, interested no one.

His urgent messages to his peers asking for coordination and cooperation on such questions as the 1964 Congolese rebellion lost their force, because he insisted on placing his proposals in the framework of the need for union government.

Since its inception Nkrumah had treated the OAU with contempt, partly because of Nkrumah's policy of union government, more importantly because Ghana could not dominate the OAU. At Cairo, Ghana offered Accra as a sight for the 1965 OAU meeting, for understandable reasons of prestige: this would be its first chance to be a part of the organization's 'in-group.'

Yet the choice of Accra posed a dilemma: Could Ghana sponsor a conference of an organization the objectives of which it rejected? This was resolved with the demand, posed almost daily in the Ghanaian press from September 1964 onwards, that the OAU effect a union government in Accra.

Hardly had Accra been selected than Nkrumah began sketching elaborate plans for a conference headquarters, the scope of which led many to conclude that Nkrumah envisaged the new buildings as an African capital. 'Jobs 600,' the remarkable £10,000,000 complex which was to be used for two weeks at the most, made Nkrumah the subject of jokes throughout the world. But these missed the point.

Obviously Ghana could ill-afford the project with the economy in such disrepair although Nkrumah did assume that the project and the conference would be a useful public diversion at a time of stress; the complex more significantly underlined the extent to which Nkrumah counted on the emergence of union government at the conference. Important objectives in the domestic sector were pushed aside, and Nkrumah told one visitor that this was done because they would be irrelevant or redundant when union government was achieved.

According to Botsio, in (an) interview, Nkrumah began at the Cairo conference itself sketching plans for the complex. Botsio himself favored the building of badly needed estate houses to house the delegates, the cost of which would have been one-tenth that of Job 600." – (Ibid., pp. 355, 357 – 358).

Nkrumah's passion for immediate continental unification will always be remembered. It was first demonstrated in a significant way when he wrote a book, *Africa Must Unite*, whose publication coincided with the first meeting of the 32 African heads of state and government who met in Addis Ababa, Ethiopia, in May

1963 and formed the Organisation of African Unity (OAU). He hoped that once they read the book, they would agree with him to unite their countries under one government – right away at that meeting or soon thereafter. They did not.

It was a severe blow to a leader who was a relentless champion of immediate continental unification and who saw himself as the embodiment of Pan-Africanism more than anybody else. As Nyerere said, Nkrumah "had tremendous contempt" for a large number of African leaders. He stated in an interview with Bill Sutherland:

"My differences with Kwame were that Kwame thought there was somehow a shortcut, and I was saying that there was no shortcut. This is what we have inherited, and we'll have to proceed within the limitations that that inheritance has imposed on us.

Kwame thought that somehow you could say, 'Let there be a United States of Africa' and it would happen. I kept saying, 'Kwame, it's a slow process.'

He had tremendous contempt for a large number of leaders of Africa and I said, 'Fine, but they are there. What are you going to do with them? They don't believe as you do – as you and I do – in the need for the unity of Africa. BUT WHAT DO YOU DO? THEY ARE THERE, AND WE HAVE TO PROCEED ALONG WITH EVERYBODY!'

And I said to him in so many words that we're not going to have an African Napoleon, who is going to conquer the continent and put it under one flag. It is not possible.

At the OAU conference in 1963, I was actually trying to defend Kwame. I was the last to speak and Kwame had said this charter has not gone far enough because he thought he would leave Addis with a United States of Africa.

I told him that this was absurd; that it can't happen.

This is what we have been able to achieve. No builder, after putting the foundation down, complains that the building is not yet finished. You have to go on building and building until you finish; but he was impatient because he saw the stupidity of the others." – (Julius Nyerere, in Bill Sutherland and Matt Mayer, eds.,*Guns and Gandhi in Africa: Pan African Insight on Nonviolence, Armed Struggle, and Liberation*, Africa World Press, 2000. The interview was also reproduced, from the book, by Chambi Chachage, "Excerpt from Interview with Bill Sutherland," Centre for Consciencist Studies and Analyses (CENSCA), 5 September 2008. See also Bill Sutherland in William Minter, Gaily Hovey, and Charles Cobb Jr., eds., *No Easy Victories: African Liberation and American Activists over a Half Century, 1950 – 2000*, New Africa Press, Trenton, New Jersey, USA, 2007).

Even Milton Obote, who was a close friend of Nkrumah, told the Ghanaian leader at the first OAU summit in Addis Ababa in May 1963 – "unity now" under one continental government could not be achieved. As he stated in an interview years later:

"I took a strong Pan African position in favour of a continental union. In May 1963, I arrived in Addis Ababa where the first conference of leaders of newly independent states was going to take place. Africa had been divided between two groups: the Monrovia group composed of conservatives, and the Casablanca group composed of the progressive radicals.

The Monrovia group was opposed to Nkrumah's proposal for an immediate creation of a union government for the whole of Africa. On the first day I arrived, my friend Kwesi Ama, a Ghanaian, came to me and said Kwame Nkrumah, the president of Ghana wanted to have lunch with me and that I should 'expect a bomb shell.' I had met Kwesi Ama in London. He was my friend and was Nkrumah's ambassador to London.

Nkrumah was the leader of African progressive opinion. We all admired him immensely. I personally admired Nkrumah immensely. He was an illustrious leader. He shaped African liberation and gave Africa a voice in world affairs. He supported liberation struggles all over Africa. So meeting him was a great honour and opportunity. People like Patrice Lumumba, Julius Nyerere, Kenneth Kaunda, all progressive African leaders looked to Nkrumah.

When we sat down to lunch, Nkrumah told me there was no conference. 'You should go back home.' He said the Monrovia group had already sabotaged the conference. I told him that we should not go back home. We should put our case to the conference on the need for African unity. And I told him that as far as I could see, there was possible success if only we could reorganise what we wanted the conference to do. Nkrumah said we wanted All-African Union Government. I told him that given the polarisation, we could not achieve that. Although we could present our case for immediate African political union, we had to be careful because we could not get the majority needed to see it through.

So we had to argue our case as a bargaining tool to get the conference to form an organisation that would work towards the creation of a continental government. I also told Nkrumah that while a continental union was a great idea, we could not wish it. We had to put in place an organisation to work towards it. During the conference, Nkrumah made a great speech on the need for a union government for Africa. He called for a constitution for an African continent government, a common market, an African currency, an African monetary zone, an African central bank and an inter-continental communication system.

I stood up in the conference, called for the creation of a strong Pan African executive and an African parliament to which all African governments must be prepared to surrender their sovereignty. This position was supported by Modibo Keita, president of Mali; Sekou Toure, president of Guinea; and the president of Egypt, Gamer Abdel Nasser. All these were my friends.

My call for immediate unity was tactics. We used the Nkrumah stand to bring others opposed to African co-operation to agree that a compromise meant building an organisation to promote the ideals of unity. Later in the conference, I suggested that since African unity cannot be achieved overnight, let us put in place an organisation to work towards the realisation of that goal. This was a compromise position between 'unity now' and the extreme position by people like President Tsiranana of Malagasy Republic (now Madagascar), Balewa and others against African co-operation.

Then Ahmed Ben Bella of Algeria took to the floor with a moving call for African liberation. He pledged 10,000 Algerian volunteers to free African nations still under colonial oppression and white minority rule. 'A Charter will be of no value to us,' he said, 'and speeches will be used against us if there is not first created a blood bank for those fighting for independence.'

I stood up and offered Uganda as a training ground for African troops to be used to liberate African countries from colonial rule and white minority rule.

Then Sekou Toure suggested that we fix a date after which 'if colonialism were not ended, African states would expel the colonial powers.'

Leopold Sedar Senghor of Senegal and Nyerere stood up and made strong recommendations on building capacity to liberate the whole of Africa.

Finally we agreed to the formation of the Organisation of African Unity (OAU) whose mandate it was to end colonial rule and work towards unity." – (Milton Obote, an excerpt from "Milton Obote: My Story," a series of interviews in which Obote was interviewed by Ugandan journalist Andrew Mwenda in Lusaka, Zambia, September – October 2004, published in *The Monitor*, Kampala, Uganda, April 2005).

Nkrumah was very impatient, and highly ambitious, in his pursuit of continental unity. And that was one of his biggest mistakes. Even if he did so with good intentions in order to see Africa united, a continent which would be powerful and prosperous as a single political entity, most of his colleagues saw him as someone who was vainglorious and power-hungry, expecting to rule Africa one day. They were not going to help him achieve his goal. They were power-hungry themselves and wanted to remain presidents of their own countries without losing power or being under somebody else even if they remained leaders in a united Africa.

More than 50 years after Nkrumah exhorted his colleagues to unite African countries under one government, which he hoped he would lead as United Africa's first president, continental unity remains elusive. Even economic integration on a continental scale remains a distant goal. He had an inordinate ambition to be Africa's "saviour" or "messiah"; hence his title, The Osagyefo, The Redeemer, leading Africa in her quest for redemption.

Also, unfortunately for Nkrumah, the books which he *did not* write – but which he claimed he wrote – are the ones which earned him a reputation as a philosopher and an anti-imperialist icon of global stature; a reputation that persists especially in the Pan-African world.

The books which were written by other people for him and which earned him that reputation were *Consciencism: Philosophy and ideology for decolonization and development with particular reference to the African Revolution*, a highly philosophical work written by Dr. Willie Abraham, and *Neo-Colonialism: The Last Stage of Imperialism* written by American and British Marxists as well as other people close to Nkrumah and living in Accra,

Ghana, during that period.

Dr. Willie Abraham also inspired one of the most renowned scholars Africa has ever produced, Ali Mazrui, who partly attributed his work, *The Africans: A Triple Heritage*, to the inspiration he draw from Nkrumah's "book," *Consciencism*. As Mazrui himself stated:

"Kwame Nkrumah also stimulated my vision of Africa as a convergence of three civilizations – Africanity, Islam and Western culture. Nkrumah called that convergence 'Consciencism.' I later called it 'Africa's Triple Heritage.' I was able to elaborate on my own concept in a BBC/PBS television series titled *The Africans: A Triple Heritage* (1986)." – (Ali A. Mazrui in IGCS Reporters, "Ali A. Mazrui, Witness to History?," op. cit.)

Since the book was not written by Nkrumah but by Willie Abraham, it is appropriate to give credit to Dr. Abraham for providing inspiration to one of the most successful documentaries about Africa by another distinguished African, Dr. Mazrui, who gave credit to Nkrumah for inspiring him in other areas as well.

Nkrumah himself had been preceded by the Liberian scholar, Dr. Edward Wilmot Blyden, in expounding the concept of Africa's triple heritage – Africanity, Islam and Western civilisation – and may actually have been inspired by him to elaborate on the convergence of these three civilisations as Blyden did in his acclaimed yet controversial book, *Christianity, Islam and The Negro Race*. In fact, a number of leading Pan-Africanists, including Nkrumah and Padmore, were greatly inspired by Blyden's ideas on unity, emancipation, African identity and heritage, just as Dr. Willie Abraham's works have provided intellectual stimulus for generation of ideas by some of Africa's prominent thinkers such as Nkrumah.

There are questions about the authorship of some of Nkrumah's other works as well, except his first book,

Towards Colonial Freedom (actually a pamphlet of about 35 pages); his second book, *Ghana: The Autobiography of Kwame Nkrumah* (encouraged by George Padmore and Padmore's partner Dorothy Pizer to write it), *I Speak of Freedom, Africa Must Unite, Class Struggle in Africa, Dark Days in Ghana, Voice from Conakry, The Struggle Continues*, and may be others.

All that may have tarnished his reputation as a thinker. But it did not diminish his stature as a continental leader who was respected and admired across Africa because of the kind of leadership he provided as a staunch Pan-Africanist. Few can match his record as an ardent advocate of continental unity under one government. Not only was he in a class by himself in that respect; no other leader pursued the same goal with the same passion and intensity as he did when he was in power. He was the first and the last.

When Nkrumah was overthrown, Nyerere paid tribute to the Ghanaian leader and even offered him asylum in spite of the differences they had on some issues vital to the wellbeing of Africa. Sekou Toure, Modibo Keita and Nasser also offered Nkrumah asylum.

Nyerere refused to recognise the new military rulers who overthrew Nkrumah and even the civilian government of Dr. Kofi Busia, Nkrumah's arch-rival, who served as prime minister from 1969 to 1972.

When his foreign affairs minister, Victor Owusu, came to Dar es Salaam in 1969 in an attempt to win recognition for the new civilian government, he was received at the airport by a low-ranking official from the ministry of foreign affairs; a deliberate snub to the leaders who had replaced Nkrumah. Owusu, together with Dr. Busia and other opposition leaders mostly from the Ashanti region, was also involved in a plot to assassinate Nkrumah in November 1958, just one year after Nkrumah led the Gold Coast to independence and became the country's first prime minister. He was going to be shot at the airport as he was getting ready to leave for a state visit to India.

The plots to assassinate Nkrumah were attributed to his despotic tendencies, ethno-regional rivalries, foreign intrigues by Western governments and intelligence agencies especially of the United States and Britain; and his determination to establish a highly centralised state that was resolutely opposed by the Ashanti who wanted a federal system under which their kingdom would retain its status as a political entity and be recognised as an autonomous unit – Obote faced the same problem from traditional centres of power, especially from the Buganda kingdom, when he decided to establish a unitary state.

Like Nyerere in Tanzania and Obote in Uganda, Nkrumah knew Ghana would be fractured along ethno-regional lines if he did not centralise power under a strong unitary state. The country had well-established traditional institutions of authority which were regionally-entrenched and needed a political party whose nationalist agenda transcended ethno-regional interests.

Nkrumah was able to provide that kind of leadership when he formed the Convention People's Party (CPP) which mobilised the masses during the struggle for independence and became the ruling party after the country emerged from colonial rule. But it also galvanised its opponents – mostly regionalists – into action, determined to undermine Nkrumah in his effort to consolidate power at the centre. As Professor Kwame Botwe-Asamoah states in his book, *Kwame Nkrumah's Politico-Cultural Thought and Policies: An African-Centered Paradigm for the Second Phase of the African Revolution*:

"In Asante, the Asantehene...and the Ashanti Confederacy Council were to form an ethno-regional political party against Nkrumah's unitary form of government in the 1956 general election (just before independence in March 1957). While Nkrumah's CPP was to enjoy strong support among the Ga-Adamge groups, the Ewes in the Trust territory were also to form an ethnic-based political party in opposition to Nkrumah's CPP. Similarly, a parochial political party was to be built and based among the northern ethnic groups in opposition to Nkrumah's CPP." – (Kwame Botwe-Asamoah, *Kwame Nkrumah's Politico-Cultural Thought and Policies: An African Centered Paradigm for the Second Phase of the African Revolution*, New York & London: Routledge, 2005, p. 93).

As a nationalist, Nkrumah had many enemies to contend with. As Professor Harcourt Fuller states in his book, *Building the Ghanaian-State: Kwame Nkrumah's Symbolic Nationalism*: Professor Harcourt Fuller states in his book, *Building the Ghanaian-State: Kwame Nkrumah's Symbolic Nationalism*:

"Nkrumah's stronghold on power, his bitter rivalry with the Asantes and other groups, and the controversial laws that he had passed jailing some of his political rivals made him a target for violence, symbolically and physically.

During his presidency, an Asante man had threatened violence against the construction of a new statue on Nkrumah in Kumasi in 1957, while his Accra statue was actually bombed in 1961. There were also several unsuccessful assassination attempts against Nkrumah himself.

In Dark Days in Ghana, Nkrumah recalled that 'members of the police and Special Branch have been involved in each of the six attacks made on my life, and have frequently ignored, and sometimes aided, the activities of people they knew were plotting to overthrow the government.'

One such assassination attempt occurred nine months after the bombing of his statue in Accra. On August 1, 1962, according to Nkrumah and Milne, a grenade attack orchstrated by 'leading police officers' in collusion with Emmanuel Obetsebi-Lamptey, 'one of the ringleaders in the plot to kill me,' was made on Nkrumah's life in Kulungugu in northern Ghana. During this unsuccessful attack, several people lost their lives, including a child, and 55 people were injured.

Other attempts on and conspiratorial plots against Nkrumah's life and coup schemes were carried out beginning with the bombing of his residence on November 10, 1955, attributed to NLM supporters; in 1958, pinned to various Opposition party officials, including J.B. Danquah, Reginald Reynolds Amponsah, Modesto Apaloo, Joe Appiah, Kofi Busia, and Victor Owusu; and on January 1, 1964, when a policeman stationed at Flagstaff House fired four shots at the president, but missed.

The various assassination attempts gave Nkrumah the motive to arrest his political opponents, as well as those in his own party whom he wanted to purge. Among those arrested were Minister of Presidential Affairs Tawia Adamafio; Foreign Minister Ako Adjei (a member of The Big Six); and Executive Secretary of the CPP Cofie Crabbe." – (Harcourt Fuller, *Building the Ghanaian-State: Kwame Nkrumah's Symbolic Nationalism*, New York: Palgrave Macmillan, 2014. See also Ahmad A. Rahman, *The Regime Change of Kwame Nkrumah: Epic Heroism in Africa and the Diaspora*, New York: Palgrave Macmillan, 2007, p. 171:

'After the fifth attempt to assassinate Nkrumah with bullets or bombs – and the deaths of 30 innocent bystanders and the wounding of over 300 – he signed the Preventive Detention Act on July 18, 1958. Nkrumah stated that the law should not alarm anybody who was not 'attempting to organise violence, terror, or civil war, or who was not acting as a fifth columnist for some foreign power.' In addition to the dead bodies, Nkrumah's intelligence agents had given him reason to suspect that certain men in the Opposition were engaging in each of these behaviors. Evidence available now proves that this was a correct assessment. Reginald Reynolds Amponsah and Modesto Apaloo were members of Parliament and leading members of the Opposition who tried to organize an anti-Nkrumah coup in 1958. A co-conspirator revealed their plot to a Nkrumah loyalist. When the police went to Amponsah's house to arrest him, at 1:00 a.m., they found him in the company of Kofi Busia, Joseph Danquah, Joe Appiah, and Victor Owusu. They were the foremost opposition figures in the country....As a unit, these men – without Danquah who died in 1965 – immediately identified with the new neo-colonial military regime soon after Nkrumah's overthrow').

The military coup against Nkrumah was preceded by a series of assassination attempts on the Ghanaian leader which began as far back as 1955; threats which may explain why he took draconian measures – non-violent – to curb the opposition and protect himself. No leader takes such threats lightly.

The opposition comprised the National Liberation Movement (NLM), the Northern People's Party (NPP) and the United Party (UP).

Nkrumah became Leader of Government Business in 1951 in preparation for independence a few years later.

Most of the attempts to assassinate Nkrumah involved bombings which claimed many innocent lives. The people who wanted to eliminate the Ghanaian leader did not target him alone. They knew the bombs and grenades they used in public places in an attempt to kill him would claim other lives, collateral damage his political enemies felt was justified even if they did not get their intended target, as long as there was a chance for him to get killed as well. Sometimes the bombings were as indiscriminate as they were bloody. No other Ghanaian leader has been the target of so much violence:

"Systematic assassination attempts on his life as well as terrorism became the language of his political opponents....(He became the target of) the most violent attacks on any president and members of his youth movement in the annals of Ghana.

While Nkrumah was resting and working from his house with his secretary and others because of a terrible cold on the evening of November 10, 1955, the house was bombed.

Between 1955 and 1958 there were several more assassination attempts on his life. Also, there was another plan to shoot him at the airport, as he was about to depart for a state visit to India.

On July 7, 1961, two bombs exploded in Accra, one wrecking Nkrumah's statue in front of the Parliament House.

The most dreadful of all the attempts on Nkrumah's life was the one that occurred at Kulungugu on August 1, 1962. Nkrumah was returning from a state visit to Upper Volta, now Burkina Faso, and had got out from his car to speak to the school children among the crowd who had gathered to greet him, when a bomb contained in a bouquet carried to him by a schoolgirl exploded. 'It killed several and injured many others. Nkrumah sustained serious injury.'

The victims' bodies bled from cuts caused by the splinters from the bomb. Nkrumah was rushed to the nearest hospital for surgery. In the process, Nkrumah refused to have any device to deaden his pain while the operation went on (*Forward Ever*: 47).

In August and September 1961, there were two separate bomb explosions on Nkrumah's life. On September 9, 1962, another bomb exploded near the 'Flagstaff House, the official residence of the President, when the Ghana Young Pioneers Orchestra Band was entertaining the audience to modern Ghanaian

Music' (Tetteh, 1999: 104). This explosion killed one person and injured others.

On September 18, 1962, two bombs again went off in Accra killing and injuring several people. One of these bomb blasts occurred in Lucas House in Accra, where nine children fell dead on the spot as their intestines gushed out of their bodies (Ibid: 104). This was followed by another bomb explosion on September 22, 1962. Consequently, a state of emergency on Accra and Tema with dusk to dawn curfew was declared.

Again, another bomb exploded on January 23, 1963, at a CPP rally in Accra Sports Stadium shortly after President Nkrumah had left the scene. This explosion killed over 20 people and more than four hundred people were injured; among the victims were children of the Young Pioneers movement (McFarland & Owusu-Ansah: ixi).

The question is, why the repeated bomb throwing at the Ghana Young Pioneers? In the words of Tetteh, the anti-Nkrumah forces saw in the Young Pioneers movement 'the source of permanent power if allowed to last for at least one generation or 35 years' (Tetteh: 93).

Having failed in their attempts to assassinate Nkrumah through the bomb blasts, the Opposition, including senior police officers, posted a police officer, Seth Ametewe, on guard duty at the Flagstaff House on January 1, 1964, to shoot him. Nkrumah recounts the incident as follows:

'It was at 1 P.M. in the garden of the Flagstaff House. I was leaving the office to go for lunch when four shots were fired at me by one of the policemen on guard duty. He was not a marksman, though his fifth shot succeeded in killing Salifu Dagarti, a loyal security officer who had run towards the would-be assassin as soon as he spotted him among the trees. The policeman then rushed at me, trying to hit me with his rifle butt. I wrestled with him and managed him to throw him to the ground and to hold him there on his back until help came, but not before he had

93

bitten me on the neck (Nkrumah, 1968: 41).'

Eventually, the repeated assassination attempts on his life caused Nkrumah to remain 'alone within himself' (Kanu: 40)." – (K. Botwe-Asamoah, *Kwame Nkrumah's Politico-Cultural Thought and Policies:*, op. cit., pp. 14 – 15).

Nkrumah also said he was able to subdue the policeman (a constable) who tried to kill him because he knew some judo techniques.

Nkrumah's opponents who tried to kill him not only supported the new military rulers; they admitted their involvement in various assassination plots to eliminate the Ghanaian leader. As Kwame Botwe-Asamoah states:

"After Nkrumah's overthrow, many in the opposition party admitted having been involved in the assassination attempts on his life.

During the Exemption Committee's hearings, Obetsebi Lamptey's name came out as having been involved in organizing several bomb explosions which caused 'the death of thirty innocent people and seriously injured many others'.

Prior to these acts of terrorism, there had been an abortive coup on November 28, 1958, carried out by Major Awhaitey; the coup was planned by R.R. Amponsah, who later became Minister of Trade in Busia's government, and others in the opposition party, to seize Nkrumah and certain members of his cabinet." – (Ibid., p. 15).

Nkrumah was overthrown nine years after he led the Gold Coast to become the first black African country to win independence. The CIA skillfully used his opponents to facilitate the coup which was masterminded by Howard T. Bane, the CIA station chief in Accra.

94

Nkrumah was the second member of The Group of Six to be overthrown, preceded by Ben Bella. Modibo Keita was next. He was overthrown in 1968. Nasser died in 1970.

Only two members of the group, Nyerere and Sékou Touré who were also close friends, remained in power. After Sékou Touré died in 1984, Nyerere was the only member of The Group of Six who remained in power. He lived long enough to witness the end of white minority rule in South Africa in 1994 in a country where Nkrumah, like Nyerere, was also highly regarded as a major inspiration to the freedom fighters and other victims of the abominable institution of apartheid.

Like Nyerere and their colleagues in The Group of Six, Nkrumah would have been thrilled to witness the end of the last white minority government on the continent when the apartheid rulers relinquished power to the black majority after the first democratic elections in the history of South Africa.

Like Nyerere, Nasser, Sekou Toure and Modibo Keita, Ben Bella also would probably have offered Nkrumah asylum but was himself overthrown eight months earlier, in June 1965, before Nkrumah was. Fidel Castro blamed Algeria's minister of foreign affairs, Abdelaziz Bouteflika, for Ben Bella's downfall. Relations between Cuba and Algeria soured as a result of the coup and remained so for several years until Castro softened his attitude towards the new military rulers in Algiers. And as Nyerere stated at a press conference in Dar es Salaam in February 1966 soon after Nkrumah was overthrown:

"What is happening in Africa? What are the coups about? The last few months have seen changes of governments in many African countries. The latest has been in Ghana. What is behind all this? Are these revolutions' intended to remove humiliation and oppression from Africa?

Let us take the latest in Ghana. The enemies of Africa are now jubilant. There is jubilation in Salisbury and Johannesburg. Even a fool could begin to wonder whether these 'revolutions' would help Africa.

What was Kwame trying to do? He stood for the liberation of Africa. There is not a single leader in Africa more committed to this than Kwame. Whom did he anger with his commitment to freedom? Certainly not Africa. He was committed to true independence. He was not merely against ordinary colonialism; he was against neocolonialism – against a colonial power going out through the political door and controlling the country through the economic door." – (Nyerere, quoted by Kwame Nkrumah, *Dark Days in Ghana*, New York: Monthly Review Press, 1968, p. 137; also in *African Quarterly*, Vol. 6, 1967, p. 279; *Pan African Journal*, Vols. 6 – 7, 1973, p. 190; Opoku Agyeman, *Nkrumah's Ghana and East Africa: Pan-Africanism and Interstate Relations*, Madison, New Jersey, USA: Fairleigh Dickinson University Press, 1992, p. 152).

Félix Houphouët-Boigny, president of the Ivory Coast who was hostile towards Nkrumah as much as he was towards Sékou Touré, also said the coup against Nkrumah was externally engineered. As he stated in an interview with *Jeune Afrique*, 4 February 1981:

"Destabilisation is not a new thing. Did you know why Idi Amin made his coup in 1972? It was not he who did it, but the British. He did not even know what he wanted himself.

It was the same in Ghana when the military overthrew Nkrumah. They [the Ghanaian coup makers] came to see me. I asked them why. They replied: 'All is not well any more.' 'Is that all?' [I asked them]. I also asked them what they were going to do; they did not know. People outside knew it for them."

Also, the Marxism Nkrumah advocated, suited to African conditions, did not last in Ghana; nor did Nyerere's *ujamaa* in Tanzania, derived from the traditional way of life and transformed into a national ideology.

It is equally true that Nkrumah's political thought can not be understood without understanding the role Marxism-Leninism played in the evolution of his thinking; it played no role in the case of Nyerere. And like Nyerere, Nkrumah remains one of the most admired leaders in the history of post-colonial Africa; he is also one of the most controversial, unlike Nyerere. But both are giants in African and world history. As Professor Mazrui stated:

"Julius Nyerere is the most enterprising of African political philosophers. He has philosophized extensively in both English and Kiswahili.

He has tried to tear down the language barriers between ancestral cultural philosophy and the new ideological tendency of the post-colonial era.

Nyerere is superbly eloquent in both English and Kiswahili. He has allowed the two languages to enrich each other as their ideas have passed through his intellect.

His concept of *ujamaa* as a basis of African socialism was itself a brilliant cross-cultural transition. *Ujamaa* traditionally implied *ethnic* solidarity. But Nyerere transformed it from a dangerous principle of ethnic nepotism into more than a mere equivalent of the European word 'socialism.'

In practice his socialist policies did not work – as much for global reasons as for domestic. But in intellectual terms Nyerere is a more original thinker than Kwame Nkrumah – and linguistically much more innovative.

Nkrumah tried to update Lenin – from Lenin's *Imperialism: The Highest Stage of Capitalism* to Nkrumah's *Neo-Colonialism: The Last Stage of Imperialism.* Nyerere translated Shakespeare into

Kiswahili instead – both *Julius Caesar* and *The Merchant of Venice*.

Nkrumah's exercise in Leninism was a less impressive cross-cultural achievement than Nyerere's translation of Shakespeare into an African language.

Yet both these African thinkers will remain among the towering figures of the twentieth century in politics and thought." – (Ali A. Mazrui in Ali. A. Mazrui, ed., *General History of Africa VIII: Africa Since 1935*, Berkeley, California, USA: University of California Press, 1993, p. 674).

In his book *On Heroes and Uhuru-Worship: Essays on Independent Africa*, Professor Mazrui also described Nyerere as "the most original thinker" among all the leaders in Anglophone Africa; Senghor in Francophone Africa. And there are those who say Nyerere was "Africa's most original thinker" among all the leaders in the post-colonial era.

In the case of Senghor, although he was ridiculed by some people for being a proponent of Négritude – he was, besides Aimé Césaire, its leading advocate on the global stage – he remains, like Nyerere, one of the most prominent thinkers and intellectuals in the history of Africa since the advent of colonial rule. And although he was a Francophile, a "black Frenchman," there is no question that he was passionate about the imperative need for black people to affirm and promote their black identity and culture. He emphasised black pride, yet without denigrating other people.

He believed it was best for the people of various cultures and civilisations to interact and work together in a world in which the contributions of black Africans would be vital to the wellbeing of humanity as a whole while retaining their identity and affirming their right to determine their own destiny.

He also made a distinction between black Africans and

Arabs in Africa in spite of the African-ness of the Arabs themselves. He felt that Arab culture had a negative impact on black Africans and had interfered with their cultural development. Still, he was not against co-existence of the two but was apprehensive of Arab intentions towards black Africa. As he stated in a conversation with the American secretary of state, Henry Kissinger, when Kissinger went to see him in Dakar, Senegal, during his African tour in 1976:

"Nigeria and Algeria try to introduce Arabs into Africa to destroy *négritude*, to impose Arab imperialism. Senegal will resist." – (Leopold Sédar Senghor, quoted by Henry Kissinger, in *Henry Kissinger: Years of Renewal*, New York: Touchstone, 1999, p. 951).

A number of other black African leaders have shared the same position through the years since independence. They have accused Arabs of trying to dominate the continent by spreading their influence from North Africa and the Middle East. They include President Hastings Kamuzu Banda of Malawi who said there was no difference between Arabs and whites in Africa:

"They are all settlers, they are both imperialists, they are both colonialists, they are both foreigners." – (Hastings Kamuzu Banda, *Opening of Lilongwe Convention, September 16, 1968*, pp. 36 – 37, quoted by Kenneth W. Grundy, *Confrontation and Accommodation in Southern Africa: The Limits of Independence*, Berkeley, California, USA: University of California Press, 1973, p. 6).

Chief Obafemi Awolowo of the Yoruba people of South-Western Nigeria, one of the three main leaders of the Nigerian independence movement – the other two were Dr. Nnamdi Azikiwe of the Eastern Region and Sir

Ahmadu Bello, the Sardauna of Sokoto, of Northern Nigeria – echoed the same sentiment expressed by Senghor regarding Arabs.

He stated in his book *Path to Nigerian Freedom* published in 1947 that President Gamal Abdel Nasser of Egypt was trying to dominate Africa. He wrote about "President Nasser's undisguised totalitarianism and territorial ambitions in Africa and the Muslim world" being a threat to black Africans.

Awolowo was not the only Nigerian leader who expressed strong feelings towards Arabs. Another one was Chief Anthony Enahoro who was also one of the country's main leaders during the independence struggle and after independence. As Ibrahim A. Gambari stated in his chapter, "The Development of African-Israeli Relations to the Yom Kippur War: Nigeria as a Case Study," in *Zionism and Arabism in Palestine and Israel*:

"Influential Southern (Nigerian) leaders such as Awolowo, head of the third major Nigerian political party, detested Nasser's Egypt and the Arab world. He did not really consider Egypt an African country and accused Nasser of 'undisguised totalitarianism (at home) and territorial ambitions in Africa and the Muslim world.'

Chief Awolowo's deputy and main spokesman on foreign affairs, Anthony Enahoro, wanted the exclusion of Arab North African countries from discussions of, and meetings about, Pan-Africanism." – (Ibrahim A. Gambari, "The Development of African-Israeli Relations to the Yom Kippur War: Nigeria as a Case Study," in Elie Kedourie and Sylvia G. Haim, eds., *Zionism and Arabism in Palestine and Israel*, Abington, Oxfordshire, UK, 1982, p. 229).

Awolowo was also the vice president of Nigeria during the civil war in the late sixties when he served as the vice chairman of the military ruling council under General

Yakubu Gowon who was the head of state.

Ugandan president, Yoweri Museveni, was equally blunt about the Arabs. He said in an interview with Stephen Sackur of HARDtalk on BBC in February 2012 that black Africans don't want Arabs to impose their culture, practices, beliefs, and way of life on them. As he stated:

"Black Africa are humble people, we never impose our views on anybody else, we are not like Europeans or Arabs who want to impose their views.

I normally tell people that when I hear Arabs talking of *haram* (something that is forbidden), something which is *haram*, I always tell them that my history of *haram* is much longer than that one of the Arabs....I don't eat very many of those things you people eat....But I keep this to myself. This is the difference with the black people....

Those jihadists (who killed more than 70 people in the Ugandan capital Kampala in July 2010) are really non-African in their attitudes. I have told you about the attitude of the black people....Our Moslems do not engage in that type of chauvinism. They keep their views to themselves, so do Christians, so do traditional groups. That's how we live in harmony....

We are ready to work together to defeat these foreigners who are coming with these chauvinistic ideas from the Middle East to implant them in our continent. In our continent, we black people, we live and let live. We never try to impose our views on anybody else."

There are other black African leaders who probably feel the same way about Arabs but do not say so publicly. They would rather express those feelings in private conversations. Yet they have found vocal expression of their position through prominent leaders such as Senghor, even though many of them, including Senghor himself, acknowledge that Arabs who are in Africa have the right to live in Africa, or simply accept the fact that they are going nowhere.

Besides being the leader of the independence movement in Senegal and his position as his country's first president and longest-ruling head of state, Senghor gained international prominence as the leading exponent of *négritude*; a position enhanced by his status as a great intellectual, philosopher, and poet.

Racial humiliation played a major role in the emergence and formation of *négritude* as a movement by black intellectuals living in France to glorify African heritage, identity, culture and way of life. Senghor was one of them.

One of its most distinctive features is the belief that interaction with other cultures is important and Africa has a lot to offer to the rest of mankind just like other societies do and is not in anyway inferior to Europe despite the fact that Europeans conquered and ruled Africans, reducing them to a subordinate status.

In defining Négritude, Senghor also emphasised the imperative need for mankind to have a civilisation of the universal, to which black Africans could make a contribution like any other people, as opposed to a universal civilisation imposed on all mankind by the members of one race. As he stated in a speech at Oxford University in October 1961:

"Paradoxically, it was the French who first forced us to seek its essence, and who then showed us where it lay...when they enforced their policy of assimilation and thus deepened our despair....

Earlier, we had become aware within ourselves that assimilation was a failure; we could assimilate mathematics or the French language, but we could never strip off our black skins or root out black souls. And so we set out on a fervent quest for the 'holy grail': our collective soul. And we came upon it.

102

It was not revealed to us by the 'official France' of the politicians who, out of self-interest and political conviction, defended the policy of assimilation. Its whereabouts was pointed out to us by that handful of free-lance thinkers – writers, artists, ethnologists, and prehistorians – who bring about cultural revolutions in France. It was, to be quite precise, our teachers of ethnology who introduced us to the considerable body of work already achieved in the understanding of Africa, by the University of Oxford.

What did we learn from all those writers, artists, and teachers? That the early years of colonization and especially, even before colonization, the slave trade had ravaged black Africa like a bush fire, wiping out images and values in one vast carnage. That Negroid civilization had flourished in the Upper Paleolithic Age, and that the Neolithic revolution could not be explained without them. That their roots retained their vigor and would one day produce new grass and green branches....

Negritude is the *whole complex of civilized values – cultural, economic, social, and political – which characterize the black peoples*, or, more precisely, the Negro-African world. All these values are essentially informed by intuitive reason, because this sentient reason, the reason which comes to grips, expresses itself emotionally, through that self-surrender, that coalescence of subject and object; through myths, by which I mean the archetypal images of the collective soul; and, above all, through primordial rhythms, synchronized with those of the cosmos.

In other words, the sense of communion, the gift of mythmaking, the gift of rhythm, such are the essential elements of Negritude, which you will find indelibly stamped on all the works and activities of the black man".... – (Leopold Sédar Senghor, "What is Negritude?," excerpt from a speech at Oxford University, England, October 1961, reprinted in *West Africa*, 4 November 1961, and in Paul E. Sigmund, Jr., ed., *The Ideologies of the Developing Nations*, New York: Frederick A. Praeger, Inc., 1963, pp. 248 – 259).

He went on to state:

"In opposition to European racialism, of which the Nazis were the symbol, we set up an 'antiracial racialism.' The very excesses of Nazism, and the catastrophes it engendered, were soon to bring us to our senses. Such hatred, such violence, above all, such weeping and such shedding of blood produced a feeling of revulsion. It was so foreign to our continent's genius: our *need to love.* And then the anthropologists taught us that there is no such thing as a pure race: Scientifically speaking – races do not exist.

They went one better and forecast that, with a mere 200 million people, we would in the end disappear as a 'black race,' through miscegenation. At the same time, they did offer us some consolation. 'The focal points of human development,' wrote Tellhard de Chardin in 1939, 'always seem to coincide with the points of contact and anastomosis of several nerve paths' – that is, in the ordinary man's language, of several races.

If, then, we were justified in fostering the values of Negritude and arousing the energy slumbering within us, it must be in order to pour them into the mainstream of cultural miscegenation (the biological process taking place spontaneously). They must flow toward the meeting point of all humanity; they must be our contribution to the civilization of the universal." – (Ibid., p. 249).

He further asserted:

"Biological miscegenation, then, takes place spontaneously, provoked by the very laws which govern life, and in the face of all policies of apartheid.

It is a different matter in the realm of culture. Here, we remain wholly free to cooperate or not, to provoke or prevent the synthesis of cultures. This is an important point. For, as certain biologists point out, the psychological mutations brought about by education are incorporated into in our genes and are then transmitted by heredity . Hence the major role played by culture.

Seen within this prospect of the civilization of the universal, the colonial policies of Great Britain and France have proved successful complements to each other, and black Africa has benefited. The policies of the former tended to reinforce the traditional native civilization. As for France's policy, although we have often reviled it in the past, it too ended with a credit balance, through forcing us actively to assimilate European civilization. This fertilized our sense of Negritude.

Today, our Negritude no longer expresses itself as opposition to European values, but as a *complement* to them. Henceforth, its militants will be concerned, as I have often said, *not to be assimilated, but to assimilate.* They will use European values to arouse the slumbering values of Negritude, which they will bring as their contribution to the civilization of the universal." – (Ibid., pp. 249 – 250).

He concluded by saying:

"Nevertheless, we still disagree with Europe: not with its values any longer (with the exception of capitalism), but with its theory of the civilization of the universal....

In the eyes of the Europeans, the 'exotic civilizations' are static in character, being content to live by means of archetypal images, which they repeat indefinitely. The most serious criticism is that they have no idea of the *pre-eminent dignity of the human person.*

My reply is this: Just as much as black Africa, Europe and its North American offspring live by means of archetypal images. For what are free enterprise, democracy, and Communism but myths, around which hundreds of millions of men and women organize their lives? Negritude itself is a myth (I am not using the word in any pejorative sense), but a living, dynamic one, which evolves with its circumstances into a form of humanism. Actually, our criticism of the [European] thesis is that it is monstrously antihumanist. For if European civilization were to be imposed, unmodified, on all peoples and continents, it could only be by force. That is its first disadvantage.

A more serious one is that it would not be *humanistic*, for it would cut itself off from the complementary values of the greater part of humanity. As I have said elsewhere, it would be a universal civilization; it would not be the civilization of the universal.

Our revised Negritude is humanistic. I repeat, it welcomes the complementary values of Europe and the white man, and, indeed, of all other races and continents. But it welcomes them in order to fertilize and reinvigorate its own values, which it then offers for the construction of a civilization which shall embrace all mankind.

The neohumanism of the twentieth century stands at the point where the paths of all nations, races, and continents cross, 'where the four winds of the spirit blow.'" – (Ibid., p. 250).

In spite of the harsh criticism Negritude has generated even from some black Africans, it has remained an influential cultural and intellectual movement. It is also Pan-Africanist in orientation. And its most prominent exponent, Senghor, is still considered to be one of Africa's towering intellectuals. He is also the most celebrated in Francophone Africa because of his intellectual dominance as a philosopher and a poet.

When the American secretary of state, Henry Kissinger, visited Africa in 1976 to meet with a number of African leaders in an attempt to end white minority rule in the countries of southern Africa, he said there were two African leaders who impressed him the most: Nyerere and Senghor as superb intellectuals and because of their different and competing visions of Africa.

Kissinger also acknowledged that Nyerere was highly independent-minded and very influential as a leader across the continent. As he stated in his book, *Henry Kissinger: Years of Renewal*, in a section entitled, "Julius Nyerere and Tanzania: The Ambivalent Intellectual":

"Tanzanian President Julius Nyerere proceeded to arrange an official reception that could not have been more cordial. The motive, however, was altogether different from Kenyatta's. Nyerere...was, at heart, deeply suspicious of American society and American intentions.

In international forums, Tanzania's ministers frequently castigated us. Nyerere would not have described friendship with the United States as a national priority; instead, he tended to think of relations with us as a necessary evil....

Brilliant and charming, Nyerere had an influence in Africa out of proportion to the resources of his country, proof that power cannot be measured in physical terms alone....Because Tanzania was involved in the armed struggle that was taking place in Rhodesia, and because of Nyerere's intellectual dominance, Nyerere would be a key to any solution....

Many of Nyerere's American admirers thought he and his colleagues were the embodiment of American values and liberal traditions. By contrast, his American critics viewed Nyerere as a spokesman for Communist ideology. Neither view was accurate. Nyerere was his own man. His idiosyncratic blend of Western liberal rhetoric, socialist practice, nonaligned righteousness, and African tribalism was driven, above all, by a passionate desire to free his continent from Western categories of thought, of which Marxism happens to be one. His ideas were emphatically his own....

For our first meeting, Nyerere, a slight, wiry man, invited me to his modest private residence. It was a signal honor, and he introduced me to his mother and several members of his family. He was graceful and elegant, his eyes sparkling, his gestures fluid.

With an awesome command of the English language (he had translated *Julius Caesar* into Swahili), Nyerere could be a seductive interlocutor. But he was also capable of steely hostility. I had the opportunity to see both these sides during my three visits to Dar es Salaam....

Nyerere was the key to the front-line states....

The two most impressive leaders I encountered on this trip, Nyerere and Senghor, were at opposite ends of the African spectrum. In a sense, they represented metaphors for varying approaches to African identity.

Nyerere was a militant who used ideology as a weapon; Senghor was an intellectual who had taught himself the grammar of power.

Nyerere considered himself as a leader of an Africa that should evolve in a unique way, separate from the currents in the rest of the world which Africa would use without permitting them to contaminate its essence. Senghor saw himself as a participant in an international order in which Africa and *négritude* would play a significant, but not isolated, role.

When all is said and done, Nyerere strove for the victory of black Africa while Senghor sought a reconciliation of cultures within the context of self-determination." - (Henry Kissinger, *Henry Kissinger: Years of Renewal*, New York: Touchstone, 1999, pp. 931 – 932, 936, 949 – 951).

After his meeting with Nyerere, Kissinger was asked at a press conference in Dar es Salaam:

"Mr. Secretary, we've just come from a press

conference with President Nyerere which was, to say the least, not encouraging for your mission. On both the Namibian and the Rhodesian questions, he said he received nothing of encouragement. In fact, on the Namibian question he said he is now less hopeful than before. Does this reflect your views on the future?...Isn't the fact alone that nothing has changed since last week an unhopeful sign?"

In his response, Kissinger said, among other things:

"The purpose of my visit here was to get clear about the views of Tanzania." - (Henry Kissinger, at a press conference in Dar es Salaam, Tanzania, in Hanes Walton Jr., Robert Louis Stevenson, and James Bernard Rosser Sr., eds., *The African Foreign Policy of Secretary of State Henry Kissinger: A Documentary Analysis*, Lanham, Maryland, USA: Lexington Books, 2007, p. 243).

Asked at a separate press conference earlier, if he thought Kissinger's mission was a failure, Nyerere responded:

"A mission of clarity is not a mission of failure."

Kissinger said Nyerere was deeply suspicious of American intentions towards Africa. But it was not just the United States Mwalimu was suspicious of; he was suspicious of world powers, especially Western, which wanted to perpetuate imperial domination of Africa.
Therefore he had reasons to be suspicious; for example, given America's track record - from supporting white minority regimes in southern Africa to undermining governments the United States did not like including engineering and supporting military coups and assassinations of African leaders, and so on.
Behind all these plots and schemes was the CIA - as is

109

still the case today - which Kissinger himself used in pursuit of American interests in Africa and elsewhere.

Some of the best examples of America's role in orchestrating military coups and killing African leaders are Nkrumah's ouster and Lumumba's assassination, both masterminded by the CIA.

The CIA even sponsored African students to study in the United States. The scholarship programme was administered by the African-American Institute based in New York City and was funded by the CIA. Many African students, including some from Tanzania, were beneficiaries of the programme, although they probably did not know they were sponsored by the CIA. All they knew was that they got scholarships from the American government to study in the United States.

The African-American Institute was established by the American government in 1954 to promote American interests in Africa. But the institute was funded by the CIA.

It was during a period when agitation for independence in Africa was at its peak; it was a continental phenomenon. American leaders knew that it was the dawn of a a new era. Colonial rule was coming to an end. Therefore, it was important for them to be on good terms with the leaders - and the people - of the countries which were emerging from colonial rule, especially at a time when the United States was locked in an ideological competition with the Soviet Union for influence in Africa and other parts of the Third World during the Cold War.

Like the United States, the Soviet Union also provided scholarships to many African students during the same period. The Soviet government even established the People's Friendship University in Moscow in 1960, renamed Patrice Lumumba University in 1961, to provide education to students from Africa and other parts of the Third World in an ideological rivalry with the West which reached its peak in the sixties, the decade of African independence. Most countries across the continent had won independence by 1968.

In the case of the United States, the African-American Institute which was in the forefront of this ideological war against the Soviet Union for influence in Africa, also published an influential magazine, *Africa Report*, to provide favourable coverage of the continent in pursuit of American interests. It was the CIA which paid for the publication of the magazine.

By providing scholarships to African students through the African-American Institute, the CIA, hence the American government, hoped that once the recipients of those scholarships returned to Africa after finishing their studies, they would help to promote American interests in their home countries, especially if they occupied high government positions, as many of them eventually did; although not all worked as stooges of the American government and the CIA. But there were those who did, including some who were not even beneficiaries of the CIA scholarship programme and who did not even go to school in the United States.

The US State Department worked closely with the African-American Institute. For example, the American ambassador to Nigeria, Donald Easum who was very close to Henry Kissinger when Kissinger was the secretary of state, later on became head of the African-American Institute and maintained close ties with African diplomats at the United Nations. The institute had its headquarters just across the street from the UN.

Even in the seventies, the CIA was busy, working on American college campuses in an attempt to recruit foreign students to work for the agency. There were reports during that period stating that the focus was on the young nations of Africa. There is no question that a number of African students were recruited by the agency.

Tanzania itself under Nyerere was of great interest to the CIA. Neighbouring Kenya was also of great interest to the CIA but for different reasons. Some of the CIA operations against Tanzania were directed from Nairobi where the agency had a large contingent, especially during the Cold War. In fact, Nairobi had the largest CIA station in East Africa.

Kenya was unabashedly pro-Western even at the expense of African interests. The CIA even paid Mzee Jomo Kenyatta a lot of money for being a loyal servant of the United States and for doing whatever the agency asked him to do. Tom Mboya was another leader who was given some money by the CIA.

Besides being a CIA stooge like Mobutu and a number of other African leaders, Kenyatta was also a tribal chauvinist who ruled Kenya with an iron fist at the expense of non-Kikuyus. He instituted a Kikuyu ethnocracy during his reign and the Kenyan state became synonymous with Kikuyu power dominated by the Kiambu Mafia.

He was such an unreconstructed tribalist that he even turned down an offer by Nyerere and Obote to be president of an East African federation because he felt that he and his people, the Kikuyu, would not have as much power and influence in such a large political unit as they had in Kenya under their ethnocratic regime. As Nyerere stated in an interview with Ikaweba Bunting of the *New Internationalist* in December 1998:

"I respected Jomo immensely. It has probably never happened in history. Two heads of state, Milton Obote and I, went to Jomo and said to him: 'Let's unite our countries and you be our head of state.' He said no. I think he said no because it would have put him out of his element as a Kikuyu Elder."

Also, Kenyatta did not support the freedom fighters in southern Africa and Guinea-Bissau the way Nyerere did and was virtually in the same camp with Kamuzu Banda in spite of being hailed as the Grand Old Man of the Kenyan – and even the African – independence movement. Even after independence, Kenya remained British property, subservient to the neocolonial master unlike Tanzania under Nyerere.

Britain, where Nyerere was given a cordial reception during his visit in 1975, did not view Tanzania favourably mainly because of its strong support for the liberation struggle in southern Africa, threatening Western interests in the region.

Nyerere will go down in history for his principled stand on a number of issues vital to the wellbeing of Africa as a whole, including his decision to sever diplomatic ties with Britain – Tanzania being the first country to do so – when the British government under Prime Minister Harold Wilson refused to use force to oust Rhodesian prime minister, Ian Smith, when he unilaterally declared independence for Rhodesia to maintain white domination of the country. Coincidentally, Mwalimu's visit to Britain took place almost ten years after Rhodesia declared independence on 11 November 1965.

Ghana under Nkrumah was the second African country to break diplomatic ties with Britain over the Rhodesian crisis; Egypt under Nasser, the third. They did so the next day after Tanzania under Nyerere ended diplomatic relations with the former colonial power.

Nyerere's stature in the Pan-African world as a giant among Pan-Africanists, besides Nkrumah, was also highlighted in 1974 when organisers of the 6th Pan-African Congress chose Dar es salaam, Tanzania, to be the venue for the conference; the first such conference to be held on African soil. The last one, the Fifth Pan-African Congress, was held in Manchester, England, in 1945. It was the most successful one and brought together a number of leaders who went on to lead their countries to independence within two decades.

Among those who attended the conference were

Nkrumah, Kenyatta, and Kamuzu Banda. Nkrumah and Kenyatta served as secretaries to the conference and were some of the main organisers of that historic meeting of Pan-Africanists from Africa and the diaspora.

The choice of Tanzania as the venue for the Sixth Pan-African Congress, almost thirty years after the last one, was an acknowledgement of Nyerere's outstanding leadership in the struggle for freedom and equality. He had already distinguished himself as the most relentless supporter of the freedom fighters in southern Africa – among all African leaders. As Professor Piero Gleijeses of Johns Hopkins University states in his book, *Conflicting Missions: Havana, Washington, and Africa, 1959 – 1976*:

"Of all the African leaders who proclaimed their support for the liberation struggle in Africa – Nkrumah, Nasser, Ben Bella, Sekou Toure – he (Nyerere) was the most committed. And by the second half of 1964, spurred by events in Zaire and the obvious failure of peaceful attempts to end white rule in southern Africa, this commitment, and his disappointment with the Western powers, was increasingly evident.

By the time Che arrived (in Tanzania in 1965), Dar es Salaam had become the Mecca of African liberation movements....Dar es Salaam 'has become a haven for exiles from the rest of Africa,' the CIA lamented in September 1964. 'It is full of frustrated revolutionaries, plotting the overthrow of African governments, both black and white'....

In September 1964, Frelimo, the movement against Portuguese rule in Mozambique, had launched the opening salvo of its guerrilla war from bases in southern Tanzania, its only rear guard.

Following Stanleyville, Nyerere had thrown his full support to the Simbas, and Tanzania had become their main rear guard and the major conduit of Soviet and Chinese weapons for them.

114

It was also the seat of the Liberation Committee of the OAU. The head offices of Frelimo and a host of other movements struggling against the white regimes in South Africa, Namibia, and Rhodesia were in Dar es Salaam." – (Piero Gleijeses,*Conflicting Missions: Havana, Washington, and Africa, 1959 – 1976*, Chapel Hill, North Carolina, USA: The University of North Carolina Press, 2002, pp. 84 and 85).

Tanzania's strong support for the freedom fighters in southern Africa was one of the main reasons Nyerere was held in very high esteem among many blacks in the United States, the Caribbean and elsewhere. Some of the most prominent organisers of the Sixth Pan-African Congress came from the United States. They included C.L.R. James (originally from Trinidad) and Amiri Baraka. They also attended the conference, as did the prominent Guyanese scholar, Walter Rodney, who was then a professor at the University of Dar es Salaam. The conference was held in Nkrumah Hall at the University of Dar es salaam. Nyerere gave the keynote address.

Nyerere had such great influence on a significant number of African Americans that when some of them decided to contribute to the development of Africa, they chose Dar es Salaam to be the headquarters of their organisation, the Pan-African Skills Center. As he stated in an interview in 1998 almost one year before he died:

"Africans who studied in the US like Nkrumah and Azikiwe were more aware of the Diaspora and the global African community than those of us who studied in Britain. They were therefore aware of a wider Pan-Africanism. Theirs was the aggressive Pan-Africanism of W.E.B. Du Bois and Marcus Garvey. The colonialists were against this and frightened of it.

After independence, the wider African community became clear to me. I was concerned about education; the work of Booker T. Washington resonated with me. There were skills we needed and black people outside Africa had them. I gave our US Ambassador the specific job of recruiting skilled Africans from the US Diaspora. A few came, like you (the interviewer, Ikaweba Bunting, who had lived in Tanzania for 25 years when he interviewed Nyerere). Some stayed; others left.

We should try to revive it. We should look to our brothers and sisters in the West. We should build the broader Pan-Africanism. There is still the room – and the need." – (Julius K. Nyerere, in an interview with Ikaweba Bunting, the *New Internationalist*, Oxford, ibid.)

Even Stokely Carmichael (renamed Kwame Ture) wanted to come to Dar es salaam when he left the United States in 1967 and moved to Africa. He said in interviews that his first choice was Tanzania where he wanted to work with the freedom fighters in Dar es Salaam but later decided to move to Conakry, Guinea, to work with Nkrumah who was living there in exile. He visited Tanzania and gave a fiery speech at the University of Dar es Salaam (see his interviews in the *Sunday News* and *The Nationalist*, Dar es Salaam, 5 – 6 November 1967).

Other blacks from the diaspora who were drawn to Tanzania and visited the country at different times included Shirley Graham Du Bois (widow of Dr. W.E.B. Du Bois), Harry Belafonte and Sidney Poitier (both prominent civil rights activists who played a major role in the civil rights movement together with Dr. Martin Luther King besides being renowned actors), Bill Sutherland who came to Tanganyika in 1963 and lived in Dar es Salaam for more than 30 years and worked with Nyerere and Kawawa; C.L.R. James, Malcolm X, Jesse Jackson, Andrew Young, Angela Davis, Robert Franklin Williams who formed a black rifle association for self defence, Charlie Cobb who was field secretary for SNNC (Student Nonviolent Coordinating Committee), Owusu Sadaukai (driving force behind African Liberation Day commemorations in the United States and president of Malcolm X Liberation University in Greensboro, North Carolina), as well as members of various nationalist groups such as the Black Panther Party (founded in Oakland, California, in October 1966), the Nation of Islam (established in Detroit, Michigan, in July 1930), the Republic of New Afrika (founded in Detroit in 1968), and the Pan-African Congress-USA (formed in Detroit in 1970).

Many of them visited or came to live in Dar es Salaam and other parts of Tanzania, inspired by Nyerere's leadership in their quest for freedom and racial equality.

Members of SNNC also attended the Youth Seminar on Racialism in Dar es Salaam from 27 – 30 April 1966 and made a passionate plea for support in their struggle for racial equality in the United States.

Malcolm X was even invited by Mwalimu Nyerere to Msasani when the African American leader visited Tanzania and other African countries in July 1964. While at Mwalimu's residence, he gave Mwalimu an album of his speech, "Message to the Grass Roots," delivered the previous year, on 10 November 1963, at a conference of black leaders in Detroit; a city with a long history of black activism since the days of Marcus Garvey and where Malcolm X spent a lot of time when he was growing up. He lived in Detroit with his eldest brother, Wilfred Little, and was nicknamed "Detroit Red." His wife also came from Detroit.

Wilfred Little, renamed Wilfred X, was himself a civil rights activist in Detroit. He died in Detroit in May 1998. He was 78. According to a report in *The New York Times*:

"Wilfred Little, who introduced his younger brother, Malcolm X, to the Nation of Islam and was a longtime official of Detroit's first Nation of Islam temple, died on Tuesday at Henry Ford Hospital here. He was 78.

Mr. Little joined the Nation of Islam in 1947 and later served as secretary and founder of Temple No. 1 in Detroit and several others in Michigan.

After the assassination of his brother in 1965, he went to work for Michigan Bell as a manager in public affairs. In 1982, the company lent him to Focus: HOPE, a civil rights and social agency, where he worked until he retired in 1988.

The eldest of the Little children, Mr. Little reared the others after their parents' died. Malcolm X was paroled into his custody in 1952 and lived with his family.

Malcolm X broke with the Nation of Islam in 1964 and was shot to death in Harlem a year later." – ("Wilfred Little, 78, Brother of Malcolm X," *The New York Times*, May 21, 1998).

Their brother Philbert Norton Little (Philbert X), born on 4 May 1923, died in Detroit on 15 February 1994.

Their half sister, Ella Little-Collins who helped raise Malcom X and took over the leadership of the Organization of Afro-American Unity after their brother Malcolm X was assassinated, died in Boston, Massachusetts, on 3 August 1996. Born in in 1914, she was the eldest child. According to a report in *The New York Times*:

"Ella L. Collins, who raised her half-brother Malcolm X, gave him money for his pilgrimage to Mecca and took over his black Muslim splinter group after his assassination, died on Saturday in a nursing home. She was 82.

Mrs. Collins had lived in a nursing home for years after suffering several strokes and diabetes, which cost her both legs.

A self-made businesswoman and civil rights activist, Mrs. Collins played an integral role in Malcolm X's life, raising him after their father died and his mother was committed to a mental hospital.

"She was the first really proud black woman I had ever seen in my life,' Malcolm X said in *The Autobiography of Malcolm X.* 'No physical move in my life has been more pivotal or profound in its repercussions.'

After Malcolm X was shot to death in February 1965 while giving a speech to 300 followers in New York City, Mrs. Collins drove to New York to identify his body. She later took charge of the Organization of Afro-American Unity, the splinter group Malcolm X founded after his 1964 falling out with the founder of the Nation of Islam, Elijah Muhammad.

Malcolm X's killers 'took something from me, something that I put a lot into,' Mrs. Collins said in an interview in *The Boston Globe Magazine* in 1992.

'He was at the point where he could become stronger than ever,' Mrs. Collins said. 'I could see Malcolm becoming the greatest black man in the history of the world.'

Mrs. Collins and Malcolm X were children of the Rev. Earl Little, a Baptist minister and organizer for Marcus Garvey's Universal Negro Improvement Association, which preached for a return of blacks to Africa....

When Mr. Little died in Lansing, Mich., in a...racially motivated killing, Malcolm X's mother, Louise, suffered a nervous breakdown and was committed to a state mental hospital.

Mrs. Collins went to Lansing in 1940 and brought Malcolm X home to Boston, officially taking custody of her half-brother when he finished the eighth grade.

In the 1950's, Mrs. Collins was recruited by Malcolm X into the Nation of Islam, then called the Temple of Islam and often known as the Black Muslims. She became active in establishing the group's Boston mosque and setting up its first day-care center.

But she broke away in 1959, became an orthodox Sunni Muslim and organized the Sarah A. Little School of

Preparatory Arts in Boston, where children were taught Arabic, Swahili, French and Spanish.

Mrs. Collins's son, Rodnell Collins, said his mother continued to be an adviser to Malcolm X, urging him 'to leave the Nation and go to orthodox Islam, to do something that was more substantial and not continue on the way he was going by putting so much energy into Elijah Muhammad's organization.'" – ("Ella Collins, 82, Relative Who Aided Malcolm X," *The New York Times*, August 6, 1996. See also "Ella Collins; Activist raised half brother, Malcolm X," the *Los Angeles Times*, August 10, 1996; "Ella Collins, Malcolm X's sister, advisor, dies," *Los Angeles Sentinel*, August 15, 1996).

And according to a report by Godfrey Hodgson, "Obituary: Ella Collins," in the *Independent*, London:

"Malcolm said of her in his Autobiography that she was 'the first really proud black woman I had ever seen.' She was 'plainly proud of her very black skin', he added, which was 'unheard of among Negroes in those days.' She was active as a businesswoman, a teacher, a civil rights worker and a religious leader.

Malcolm, whose original surname was Little, was the son of the Rev Earl Little, a Baptist preacher and an organiser for Marcus Garvey's United Negro Improvement Association in Michigan. Earl Little was a jet-black-skinned man, four of whose six brothers had been killed by white men, one by lynching.

Ella Collins was one of Earl Little's three children by a previous marriage. She was brought up in Georgia, then moved to Boston. Earl Little married again, a light-skinned woman from Grenada in the West Indies, Louise, whose father was white.

In 1931 Earl Little was killed in a streetcar accident. His son Malcolm believed he was murdered by a white vigilante group called Black Legion. For a while Louise

Little struggled to bring up her children but, after a relationship with a man broke up, she had a breakdown and she spent the last 24 years of her life in a mental hospital in Kalamazoo, Michigan. In 1940 Malcolm's half-sister Ella Little Collins appeared like a guardian angel and invited the boy, then aged 15, to stay with her in Boston.

Ella Little grew up in Georgia, then moved to New York, where she became secretary to the brilliant but frequently outrageous black congressman, Adam Clayton Powell, who represented Harlem. She later moved to Boston, where she managed her mother's grocery store and invested in house property, which she let out as rooming houses. She lived in Waumbeck Street in what was known as Sugar Hill, the most prosperous part of Roxbury, the black neighbourhood in Boston. To her half-brother it seemed she was 'busily involved in dozens of things,' including clubs and civil rights groups.

Malcolm was thrilled by the bright lights of Boston and reassured by his half-sister's strength and confidence. When he went back to Lansing, he wrote to her, saying he wanted to move to Boston and live with her. She arranged for official custody of the boy (now a ward of the state) to be transferred from Michigan to Massachusetts.

'No physical move in my life,' Malcolm wrote later, 'has been more pivotal or profound in its repercussions. All praise is due to Allah that I went to Boston when I did. If I hadn't, I'd probably be a brainwashed black Christian.'

At about that time Ella Collins broke up with her second husband, a soldier called Frank. (Her first husband was a doctor, and she later married for a third time.) She had paid, with the money she made from her rented property, for several members of the family to move from Georgia to Boston.

Since her days working for Adam Clayton Powell, Collins had been committed to the struggle for civil rights, but in the 1950s Malcolm persuaded her to join the Nation of Islam, the so-called 'black Muslims,' founded by Elijah Muhammad, another disciple of Marcus Garvey. She helped to establish the Nation's mosque in Boston and a day-care centre attached to it.

When Malcolm became interested in Islam world-wide, as opposed to the Elijah Muhammad version of it, it was Ella Collins who paid for his first visit to Mecca. When he said he wanted to make the pilgrimage, she replied simply, 'How much do you need?', although she herself as a Muslim convert would have liked to make the journey, and she and Malcolm had disagreed on many questions.

They talked all night about his visit, which was to take him not only to Mecca but to Cairo, Beirut and West Africa, and marked a critical change in his political orientation in the direction of a less confrontational, more positive attitude.

In 1959 she left the Nation of Islam and became an orthodox Sunni Muslim. She set up the Sarah A. Little School of Preparatory Arts in Boston, where children were taught Arabic, Swahili, French and Spanish as well as other subjects.

When Malcolm was killed, she drove from Boston to New York to identify the body and helped organise the funeral, a major event in the development of a separatist consciousness among African Americans and also in alerting white opinion to the changing mood among urban blacks.

She told an interviewer a few years ago that Malcolm's murderers 'took something from me that I put a lot into.' Malcolm, she believed, was 'at the point where he could become stronger than ever. I could see Malcolm becoming the greatest black man in the history of the world.'

In recent years she suffered a number of strokes and both her legs had to be amputated as a result of diabetes. She left a son, two grandchildren, three brothers and a sister.

Ella Little (Ella Collins), civil rights activist: born 1914; married three times (one son); died 3 August 1996."
– (Godfrey Hodgson, "Obituary: Ella Collins," the *Independent*, London, 6 August 1996).

Another one of their brothers, Robert Langdon Little, died at a hospital in Lansing, Michigan, on 23 November 1999. He was 61. He was born on 31 August 1938 in Lansing and was the youngest in the family. He was the first person in his family to go to college. He earned a master's degree in social work and criminal justice from Michigan State University in East Lansing in 1963. He said it was his brother Malcolm X who encouraged him to finish his education. Malcolm X was 13 years older than he was.

Reginald Little (Reginald X), another brother, died in Grand Rapids, Michigan, on 12 July 2001. He was born on 23 August 1927.

One of their sisters, Yvonne (Evonne) Little Jones-Woodward, died in Grand Rapids, Michigan, on 21 July 2003. She was 73 and was a civil rights activist. According to a report in *The Grand Rapids Press*:

"Yvonne Woodward, sister of the late black activist Malcolm X, died Monday of complications from lung cancer, relatives said. Ms. Woodward, who took up the mantle of speaking out against racism later in her life, was 73....

Ms. Woodward, like her seven siblings, spent a lifetime overcoming tragedy, beginning with the death of her father, the Rev. Earl Little. Later, her mother was put in the state mental facility in Kalamazoo. The eight children were split apart and sent to various foster families in the Lansing area.

'It had a big impact on her life,' said her son, Steve Jones, 50....

In 1948, she became the first black telephone operator

in Grand Rapids...for Michigan Bell Co. She previously was the first black operator in Lansing....

'She knew if she didn't do the right thing, it would take years for them to take a chance to hire another black operator,' Jones said. 'In Grand Rapids, the operators took a vote to see if the girls were willing to have a 'Negro' work with them. The vote was unanimous except one vote ... and my mother found out who she was and won her over.'

Another brother, Reginald Little, died in Grand Rapids in 2001.

Two siblings remain: Wesley Little, 75, of Detroit, and Hilda Little, 80, of Woodland Park...in Newaygo County, Michigan.

Ms. Woodward also is survived by her three children, Deborah Jones, 52, of Grand Rapids, Steve Jones, of Woodland Park, and Shawn Durr, 37, of Grand Rapids....

In a speaking event at East Grand Rapids High School eight years ago, she spoke about how her parents instilled the crusading spirit that later emerged in her brother, Malcolm X." – (Steven Harmon, "Sister of Malcolm X dies at 73," *The Grand Rapids Press*, Grand Rapids, Michigan, USA, July 23, 2003).

Another sister who was the second-born child and last surviving member of the family, Hilda Florice Little, died at a hospital in Grand Rapids, Michigan, on 5 April 2015. Born on 22 October 1921, she was 93. According to her obituary, "She was preceded in death by her parents; her brothers Wilfred Little, Philbert Little, Shabazz 'Malcolm X,' Reginald Little, Wesley Little and Robert Little; and her sister Yvonne Woodward."

Like her siblings, she was an embodiment of endurance and determination that was best reflected by the work of Malcolm X who was assassinated on 21 February 1965 at the age of 39.

Malcolm X knew he had enemies in the Nation of

Islam who wanted to kill him. But he also knew their limitations and capabilities. He said he knew their tactics because "I invented some of those tactics myself."

He knew Black Muslims were not the ones who poisoned him at a hotel in Cairo. He knew it was not Black Muslims who stopped him from going to Paris, France, at the last minute on 9 February 1965, twelve days before he was assassinated. When the French immigration officials told him the American embassy was behind it, he responded by saying, "I didn't know that France was a satellite of the United States."

He was expelled from France.

He knew he was targeted for elimination by the American government, not just by the Black Muslims. The Nation of Islam itself was infiltrated by the FBI; so were the Black Panthers, the Republic of New Afrika, the civil rights movement in which photojournalist Ernest C. Withers (1922 – 2007), who was a friend of Dr. Martin Luther King and was so close to him, was a paid FBI informer, among others.

John X Ali, the national secretary of the Nation of Islam and the second most powerful man in the organisation after Elijah Muhammad himself, was an undercover FBI agent. There was even a time when John X Ali lived with Malcolm X and was supposed to be a close friend of his. He also had a meeting with Malcolm X's assassins the night before they killed the former Black Muslim leader who was the most popular and most articulate spokesman of the Nation of Islam, eclipsing its leader, Elijah Muhammad. There were several undercover FBI agents in the Nation of Islam who worked with John X Ali.

Also, one of Malcolm X's bodyguards, Gene Roberts, was an undercover agent for the FBI and the New York Police Department.

As an indefatigable fighter for the freedom of his people, he incurred the wrath of the American government in a country where racial discrimination and other forms of injustices against blacks had official sanction in some states, especially in the south, and *de facto* segregation was a nationwide phenomenon despite professions to the contrary. He said there is no difference between a Republican wolf and a Democratic fox.

He launched an initiative to bring the United States before the United Nations on charges of racism against blacks. He drew parallels between what was going on in the United States and in South Africa, contending that if the apartheid regime can be accused of practising racism, there is no reason why the American government should not face the same charge before the UN. Nine African countries agreed to raise the matter before the UN General Assembly. They included Ghana, Egypt, Guinea and Tanzania. But the matter was not brought up because of strong American resistance to the initiative.

Malcolm X died tireless and undefeated; a spirit he and his brothers and sisters inherited from their parents.

Their father, Earl Little, was a Baptist preacher and follower of Marcus Garvey and helped propagate his teachings. Their mother, Louise Helen Little, was an immigrant from Grenada. She suffered a nervous breakdown in 1938 and spent almost 25 years in a mental institution in Kalamazoo, Michigan. Her children, including Malcolm X, helped to get her released in 1963. She died in Lansing, Michigan, in 1991. She was 94.

Their father was killed by racists in Lansing, Michigan, in 1931 because of his strong stand against racial injustices perpetrated against blacks. Just two years before he was killed, his house was burned by racists in 1929.

Years later, Malcolm X recalled with bitterness in his work, *The Autobiography of Malcolm X*, what happened on that day, saying when the firemen came, they did not put "one drop of water" on the house when it was burning. They just sat there. As he put it:

"The firemen came and just sat there without making any effort to put one drop of water on the fire."

He went on to state: "The same fire that burned my father's home still burns my soul," in pointed reference to the racial injustices he continued to suffer throughout his life. It was a collective sentiment shared by millions of black Americans.

Malcolm X also spoke at the OAU summit in Cairo in July 1964. He almost died in Cairo when his food was poisoned at the hotel where he was staying. The CIA followed him throughout his African trip. The American secretary of state, Dean Rusk, also complained about Malcolm X and his trips to Africa – he visited the continent twice in 1964, also twice in 1959 – saying he was telling Africans how bad the United States was in terms of race relations, mistreating blacks, and even compared it to apartheid South Africa, contending that there were striking similarities between the two as racist countries.

Even some African leaders and diplomats were subjected to racial indignities in the United States. One of the most well-known incidents involved Ghana's minister of finance, Komla Gbedemah, who was the second most powerful man in Ghana after Nkrumah himself.

He was in the United States in October 1957 to seek financial assistance for the construction of the Akosombo Dam on the Volta River the country needed to generate electricity vital to the country's rapid economic development envisaged by Nkrumah and was denied service at a Howard Johnson's restaurant in Dover, Delaware.

He was travelling in a car from New York to Washington, D.C., to find out how he could get some help to finance the Volta River project. After he was denied service at the restaurant – he wanted to buy a glass of orange juice – he told the manager he was going to make

127

sure the incident got international coverage. It did. As Professor Thayer Watkins of San Jose State University in California stated in "The Volta River Project in Ghana":

"Nkrumah prevailed upon President Dwight Eisenhower to use his personal influence to persuade Henry Kaiser to put together a consortium of aluminum companies to build an aluminum smelter in Ghana. Kaiser and the consortium were willing to build the aluminum smelter only if the price of electricity was extremely low. Later that low price was criticized as exploitative but it had to be that low to induce the aluminum producers to build the smelter in the first place.

There is an interesting anecdote concerned with how the Volta River Project was resurrected. Komla Gbedemah, the Minister of Finance and a top leader of Ghana second only to Nkrumah, was traveling in the U.S. in 1957. He and his secretary, an African American, stopped for breakfast at a roadside restaurant in Delaware and ordered orange juice. The waitress said she could not serve him because he was black. Gbedemah asked to see the manager who told him the same thing. Gbedemah then told the manager:

'The people here are of a lower social status than I am but they can drink here and we can't. You can keep the orange juice and the change, but this is not the last you have heard of this.'

The next day the incident was headline news around the world.

President Eisenhower invited him for breakfast the next day. Eisenhower asked Gbedemah what he was visiting in America for and Gbedemah told him it was to try to find funding for the Volta River Dam. Eisenhower asked Vice President Richard Nixon to help arrange financing."

Gbedemah was, like Kofi Baako, one of Nkrumah's most trusted lieutenants. He later turned against Nkrumah and even got support from the United States in an attempt to overthrown him. Unlike Gbedemah, Baako remained loyal to Nkrumah until the end. Colin Legum, in his book *Africa Since Independence*, stated that Baako was the only cabinet member under Nkrumah who was not corrupt:

"Here are a few examples of the beginnings of corruption in two new African states which I personally observed....

Nkrumah discovered that some of his ministers were accepting payoffs from foreign building firms for contracts. Instead of cracking down on this practice, which would not have gone down well with some of his colleagues, Nkrumah institutionalized payoffs by declaring that 10 percent of all bribes were to be paid over to the party. This opened the way for extensive bribe-taking in Ghana, which is known to have been resisted by only one senior minister, Kofi Baako.

My next example comes from Nigeria, where, almost from the beginning of independence, a thrusting entrepreneurial class engaged in sophisticated scams." – (Colin Legum, *Africa Since Independence*, Bloomington, Indiana, USA: Indiana University Press, 1999, pp. 41 – 42).

Although Gbedemah fell out with Nkrumah, he is still remembered as one of the architects of Ghana's independence movement and as the one who obtained American assistance for the construction of the Akosombo Dam Nkrumah wanted so much to build. The racial incident in which he was involved when he was denied service at a restaurant in the United States also earned him a place in history, highlighting the injustices black Americans suffered while the United States preached freedom and equality abroad without fully practising it at home.

Malcolm X knew about such incidents and the racial indignities some African leaders and students suffered, including diplomats accredited to the United States and to the UN. Adam Clayton Powell, a black US congressman representing Harlem, even introduced a bill in Congress in May 1961 which required imposing heavy fines and other stiff penalties on anyone who discriminated against foreign dignitaries including ambassadors as well as other officials from other countries because of their racial identity.

Powell was one of the people Malcolm X greatly admired because of his strong stand against racial injustices in the United States. The FBI also had a file on the congressman. The authorities considered him to be a militant.

Malcolm X was also under constant FBI surveillance. When he returned to New York in December 1964 after his African trip, FBI agents were at the airport waiting for him and commented on his close ties to Tanzania. An FBI report stated that Malcolm X got into a car with a diplomatic license plate which was traced to "the new nation of Tanzania." The United Republic of Tanganyika and Zanzibar, formed on 26 April 1964, was renamed the United Republic of Tanzania on October 29th in the same year.

FBI agents followed him and said the car took him to the residence of the Tanzanian ambassador to the United Nations.

Many African Americans had very high regard for Tanzania when the country was under the leadership of Nyerere as much as they did for Ghana during Nkrumah's presidency. They considered the two leaders, together with Ahmed Sekou Toure, to be the true embodiment of Pan-Africanism. In fact, it was Nyerere, more than any other African leader, who strongly supported Malcolm X in

130

Cairo in July 1964 to bring up the subject of racial oppression of black people in the United States at the OAU conference so that it could be addressed by the leaders at the summit.

They discussed it and passed a resolution condemning racial discrimination against the "people of African descent in the United States." They also warned that relations between African countries and the United States would deteriorate if such injustices continued. It was Nyerere who presented that resolution and who was the driving force behind it.

Malcolm X spoke at the OAU summit as a representative of the Organisation of Afro-American Unity (OAAU) which he formed after he left the Nation of Islam in March 1964.

He said in one of his speeches in the United States that the OAAU was patterned after "our mother organisation," the OAU.

Also, it was Nyerere who was responsible for another resolution which became one of the cardinal principles of the OAU. He presented a resolution which stated that African countries should maintain the boundaries they inherited at independence to avoid chaos and conflict which could result from any attempt to change those borders as Somalia attempted to do by claiming Djibouti, parts of northeastern Kenya and the Ogaden region of Ethiopia which were mostly inhabited by ethnic Somalis in order to create Greater Somalia. As Nyerere himself stated:

"In 1964 we went to Cairo to hold, in a sense, our first summit after the inaugural summit. I was responsible for moving that resolution that Africa must accept the borders which we inherited from colonialism; accept them as they are. The resolution was passed by the organisation (OAU) with two reservations: one from Morocco, another from Somalia." – (Nyerere, "Reflections," in Godfrey

Mwakikagile, *Nyerere and Africa: End of an Era*, 2010, p. 556).

Like Somalia, Morocco also had territorial ambitions of annexation. The Moroccan king claimed what was then Spanish Sahara to be an integral part of Morocco.

Despite its good intentions, Nkrumah did not like the resolution that was presented by Nyerere to maintain the territorial integrity of African countries. He saw it as a deliberate attempt to keep Africa balkanised if the countries continued to maintain their sovereignities instead of submerging them in a larger entity under one government – of a United States of Africa – as he strongly urged his colleagues to do.

And Nyerere's success in helping Malcolm X at the OAU summit in Cairo for the organisation to officially acknowledge and condemn racial discrimination against blacks in the United States earned him even more respect and admiration among African Americans as an ally in their struggle for racial equality.

Although Nyerere was greatly admired by a significant number of African Americans, it was Nkrumah who had a longer relationship with the black community in the United States. Nkrumah's relationship with African Americans started in the late thirties when he was a student there. And he maintained those ties after he returned to the Gold Coast (renamed Ghana after independence).

He even invited some of them to attend Ghana's independence celebrations on 6 March 1957. They included civil rights leaders such as Martin Luther King, some of his classmates at Lincoln University (a black school), and even a black teacher from California whom he did not know. She wrote Nkrumah saying she wanted to take part in the independence celebrations and Nkrumah invited her to Ghana.

Black people in the United States had a profound

influence on Nkrumah in a way they did not on Nyerere. In Nkrumah's case, not only did his relationship with black Americans start when he was a student in the United States; he maintained strong ties with some of them even after he became president of Ghana; best exemplified by the invitation he extended to Dr. W.E.B. Du Bois and his wife, asking them to go and live in Ghana.

But it was the teachings of Marcus Garvey (a Jamaican known for his "Back to Africa" movement), more than anything else, which had the biggest impact on Nkrumah in terms of political awakening, as he himself stated in his book, *Ghana: The Autobiography of Kwame Nkrumah* first published in 1957, the same year he led his country to independence.

Years later, he paid tribute to Marcus Garvey in a speech during Ghana's independence celebrations stating that the end of colonial rule for the Gold Coast, now Ghana, was the culmination of cumulative efforts - what Garvey and others had fought for in the past. As Professor Ali Mazrui stated in his book, *Towards a Pax Africana: A Study of Ideology and Ambition*:

"At a state dinner to mark Ghana's independence many years later, Nkrumah had occasion once again to recall Garvey. But just before he mentioned Garvey's name to illustrate a point, he invoked the dramatic device of asking the band to play Ghana's new national anthem. Then he made his point, saying:

'Here I wish I could quote Marcus Garvey. Once upon a time, he said, he looked through the whole world to see if he could find a government of a black people. He looked around, he did not find one, and he said he was going to create one. But here today the work of Rousseau, the work of Marcus Garvey, the work of Aggrey, the work of Caseley Hayford, the work of these illustrious men who have gone before us, has come to reality at this present moment.'

Earlier in the speech Nkrumah had reaffirmed Pan-Negroism in the following terms:

'There exists a firm bond of sympathy between us and the Negro peoples of the Americas. The ancestors of so many of them come from this country. Even today in the West Indies, it is possible to hear words and phrases which come from various languages of the Gold Coast.'

In the history of Pan-Africanism the most important Negroes of the Americas remained George Padmore from the West Indies and W.E.B. Du Bois from the United States. To these historic figures Ghana opened her doors on attainment of independence. They died citizens of Ghana. The whole phenomenon was a 'Back to Africa' event of unique symbolism." – (Ali A. Mazrui, *Towards a Pax Africana: A Study of Ideology and Ambition*, op. cit., pp. 60 – 61).

George Padmore had great influence on Nkrumah as much as Dr. W.E.B. Du Bois and C.L.R. James did. In fact, he played a major role in formulating and shaping Ghana's foreign policy and was bitterly resented by prominent Ghanaians such as Dr. Robert Gardiner for the great influence he had on Nkrumah as his adviser on African affairs and even contemplated leaving Ghana because of that. Dr. Gardiner was the head of Ghana's civil service during that time, the first to hold the position soon after the country won independence, and later served as the Under-Secretary-General and Executive Director of the UN Economic Commission for Africa (ECA) from 1961 to 1975.

Padmore wrote – among other works – a highly influential book, *Pan-Africanism or Communism? The Coming Struggle for Africa*, first published in 1956, shortly before Ghana won independence the following year. Oscar Kambona, then a student in London, wrote Padmore in 1957 to congratulate him for writing the book. He saw it as a monumental achievement comparable to Nkrumah's success in leading the Gold Coast to independence:

"The young Oscar Kambona, then a law student in London, summarized the importance of Padmore's *Pan-Africanism or Communism?* by writing him in 1957 that his 'achievement on writing this book is on the same level as the achievement of Dr. Kwame Nkrumah in bringing his country to independence.'" – (Oscar Kambona to George Padmore, 19 January 1957, in Padmore library, Accra, Ghana, quoted by Willard Scott Thompson, *Ghana's Foreign Policy, 1957 – 1966: Diplomacy Ideology, and the new State,* Princeton, New Jersey, USA: Princeton University Press, 1969, p. 22).

Kambona even attended the All African People's Conference in Accra, Ghana, in 1958, organised by Nkrumah.

He later became very close to Nkrumah. He maintained close ties with the Ghanaian leader when he was Tanzania's minister of defence and external affairs at a time when Nkrumah was trying hard to undermine Nyerere. Kambona himself was nurturing his own ambition to replace Nyerere as president of Tanzania.

Nkrumah tried to accomplish his mission by cultivating ties with some people in the Tanzanian government who were close to Nyerere and who would be willing to work with him against the Tanzanian leader:

"East Africa was high on Nkrumah's list of subversion priorities. At one point, early in 1965, an attempt was made to recruit two sources close to Tanzania's President Julius Nyerere to 'exploit the political contradictions in the

135

East African area.'" – (*Atlas*, a journal, Worley Publishing Company, New York, 1966, p. 22).

Kambona was probably was one of them, considering the close ties he had with Nkrumah and his own ambition to be the next president of Tanzania.

He became a bitter opponent of Nyerere after he left Tanzania in July 1967 and was the mastermind of a plot to overthrow the Tanzanian leader. The coup was to take place in October 1969, when Kambona was living in exile in London, but was discovered by Tanzania's intelligence service before it could be carried out.

He died in London in 1998. Nyerere also died in London the following year. George Padmore, who was admired by both, also died in London 40 years before Nyerere did.

After Ghana became independent, Nkrumah invited Padmore to Accra to be his adviser on African affairs. And like Dr. W.E.B. Du Bois, Padmore died a Ghanaian and was buried in Accra, Ghana. He died in London in 1959.

Had he lived longer until Nkrumah was overthrown, it is very much possible he could have moved to Tanzania (as much as Dr. W.E.B. Du Bois could have) which was the next choice for a number of people who were supporters of Nkrumah but who had to leave Ghana after the Ghanaian leader was overthrown. They included freedom fighters from southern Africa who were being trained in Ghana when Nkrumah was in power. They were flown to Dar es Salaam within days of Nkrumah's ouster; some of their expenses – for plane tickets and so on – paid by a number of Afro-Americans living in Accra.

Dar es Salaam was the obvious destination for the freedom fighters who had been expelled from Ghana by the new military regime – which was subservient to the United States in a disgusting way – because it was the headquarters of the OAU Liberation Committee in a country that had been chosen by other African leaders to provide sanctuary for the freedom fighters; a clear acknowledgement of Nyerere's stature as a highly influential leader and strong supporter of the liberation movements in southern Africa.

Ghana under Nkrumah ended up being the headquarters of the OAU Defence Committee based in Accra, but important only for its symbolism since it was largely ineffective, unlike the Liberation Committee based in Dar es Salaam. Nkrumah tried strenuously to have Accra chosen by the OAU to be the headquarters of the Liberation Committee but other African leaders chose Dar es Salaam, instead.

Still, it was in acknowledgement of Nyerere's and Nkrumah's stature as giants in the pantheon of Pan-African leadership that their countries were chosen by their colleagues to be the headquarters of the two OAU committees even though one of those committees was important only for its symbolic value – yet a highly significant gesture to Nkrumah as an embodiment of Pan-Africanism and a trail blazer in the African independence struggle when he led the Gold Coast to become the first black African country to emerge from colonial rule; also befitting a leader who, during the Congo crisis in 1960, was the first to propose formation of an African High Command to defend the continent.

The sacrifices Tanzania – under the leadership of Nyerere – made to the liberation struggle in southern Africa will always be remembered even if they are overlooked or ignored by some of the people who were helped during those days.

One example of the contributions Tanzania made to the liberation struggle was explained by a British journalist, David Martin, after he interviewed Nyerere one day:

"I remember one day sitting in his office questioning that a number of African countries had not paid their subscriptions to the OAU Liberation Committee Special

Fund for the Liberation of Africa. He looked at me for some moments, thoughtfully chewing the inside corner of his mouth in his distinctive way. Then, his decision made, he passed across a file swearing me secrecy as to its contents. It contained the amount that Tanzanians, then according to the United Nations the poorest people on earth, would directly and indirectly contribute that year to the liberation movements. I was astounded; the amount ran into millions of US dollars.

It was the practice among national leaders in those days to say that their countries did not have guerrilla bases. Now we know that Tanzania had many such bases providing training for most of the southern African guerrillas, who were then called 'terrorists' and who today are members of governments throughout the region.... Tanzania was also directly attacked from Mozambique by the Portuguese. But, in turn, each of the white minorities in southern Africa fell to black majority political rule and Nyerere saw his vision for the continent finally realized on 27 April 1994 when apartheid formally ended in South Africa with the swearing in of a new black leadership." – (David Martin, "A Candle on Kilimanjaro," in *Southern African Features*, 21 December 2001).

Then there was the enormous sacrifice Tanzania made in the liberation wars in terms of lives. The country lost soldiers, men and women, so that others could live and win their freedom in the countries of southern Africa still under white minority rule. They did. All that was done because of Nyerere.

Nkrumah also wanted to play a major role, as a liberator, in the countries of southern Africa still under white minority rule. His desire to send Ghanaian troops to Rhodesia to remove the white minority rulers from power contributed to his ouster.

Ghanaian soldiers even conducted military exercises ostensibly in preparation for the mission. Instead, the

138

military exercises were in preparation for a coup against Nkrumah which took place on 24 February 1966 less than two months after the white minority rulers of Rhodesia declared independence.

And while Nkrumah came up with the daring idea – although premature and impractical – of invading Rhodesia, using his army to topple the white minority regime which had illegally declared independence, it was Nyerere who was the strongest critic of Britain for its unwillingness and refusal to use its troops to end the rebellion in its colony of Rhodesia. As Professor Ali Mazrui stated in his lecture at the University of Ghana in 2002:

"Julius K. Nyerere of Tanzania was regarded as revolutionary partly because he became the most radical voice of Pan-Africanism after the overthrow of Nkrumah. Nyerere was also regarded as a revolutionary innovator in socialism and a left-wing experimentalist....

In the debates between incremental Pan-Africanism and rapid unification Nkrumah found a rival in Julius K. Nyerere of Tanzania....

Nyerere's reputation came much later as a symbol of post-independence African radicalism rather than of pre-independence African militancy....the torch of African radicalism, after the coup which overthrew Nkrumah in 1966, was in fact passed to Nyerere.

The great voice of African self-reliance, and the most active African head of government in relation to liberation in Southern Africa from 1967 until the 1980s was in fact Julius Nyerere....

In reality Nkrumah and Nyerere had already begun to be rivals as symbols of African radicalism before the coup which overthrew Nkrumah. Nkrumah was beginning to be suspicious of Nyerere in this regard.

The two most important issues over which Nyerere and Nkrumah before 1966 might have been regarded as rivals for continental pre-eminence were the issues of African liberation and African unity.

It was soon clear that the most difficult problems of decolonization were likely to be the Portuguese dependencies and Rhodesia.

The Organization of African Unity, when it came into being in May 1963, designated Dar es Salaam as the headquarters of liberation movements.

The choice was partly determined by the proximity of Dar es Salaam to southern Africa as the last bastion of colonialism and white minority rule. But the choice was also determined by the emergence of Nyerere as an important and innovative figure in African politics.

Nkrumah's Ghana did make a bid to be the headquarters of liberation movements but Nkrumah lost the battle. If the reason had simply been that Dar es Salaam was closer to the arenas of colonial conflict, Nkrumah might have accepted this more readily.

But at least as important a reason for the success of Dar es Salaam in being designated the Mecca of liberation movements was the fact that Nkrumah, by mid-1963, had already accumulated several enemies, especially in French-speaking Africa. Nkrumah's encouragement of dissidents from neighboring countries, although it had yet to reach the proportions it reached in 1965, had begun to rear its head as a grievance among neighbours....

As the years went by Nkrumah felt that freedom fighters were not simply those who were fighting against colonial rule but also those who were fighting against their own African neo-colonial regimes. This was domestic revolution versus anti-colonialism first phase.

The hospitality he extended to rebels from his French-speaking neighbours, and even to dissidents from Nigeria, made him less and less acceptable as a patron of major Pan-African ventures, especially if these depended on the blessing of the Organization of African Unity. In 1963 suspicion of Nkrumah was already strong enough to make it unlikely that Accra, Ghana, would be acceptable as the official liberation capital of the African continent. Nkrumah strongly resented this reaction.

The other major arena in which Julius Nyerere was a rival to Nkrumah was the arena of regional integration. For years Nkrumah had been the eloquent voice of Pan-Africanism and the symbol of the continent's quest for greater integration. On a more modest scale Nkrumah had even attempted to lead a union first between Guinea and Ghana, and later between Guinea, Ghana and Mali....But these...attempts at unification which Nkrumah had led proved abortive.

Then in 1961 and 1962 it appeared as if Nyerere was going to succeed in leading the East African countries to a regional federation of Tanzania, Kenya and Uganda. By June 1963 the three heads of government in East Africa – Kenyatta, Obote, and Nyerere – felt confident enough to announce plans to form an East African federation before the end of the year.

In 1960 Nyerere had already stolen the limelight on federalism in Africa by announcing his readiness to delay Tanganyika's independence until Kenya and Uganda became independent if this would facilitate the formation of an East African federation. In June 1963 Kenya was still not independent, but the other two had attained theirs.

This time the clarion call was not for Tanzania to delay its independence but for Kenya to speed up its own timetable of decolonization. The British were called upon to grant Kenya independence by December 1963 so as to enable it to join in a federation with the other two.

It was in this sense that Nyerere had by that time become a symbol of African unification, apparently standing a greater chance of success in effective inter-territorial integration than Nkrumah had stood in his own ventures with Guinea and Mali.

Nkrumah's reaction was not overly subtle. He propounded a new thesis that sub-regional unification of the kind envisaged in East Africa was in fact simply 'Balkanization writ large.'

Further, the enterprise was likely to compromise the bigger ambition of a continental union in Africa. It was a case of the good being the enemy of the best – and East Africans who accepted the minimally good achievement of sub-regional federation would no longer have the incentive to embark on continental union as a more effective bulwark against neo-colonialism and poverty. Nkrumah pointed out that his own country could not very easily join an East African federation. This proved how discriminatory and divisive the whole of Nyerere's strategy was for the African continent.

Nyerere treated Nkrumah's counter-thesis with contempt. He asserted that to argue that Africa had better remain in small bits than form bigger entities was nothing more than 'an attempt to rationalize absurdity.'

He denounced Nkrumah's attempt to deflate the East African federation movement as petty mischief-making arising from Nkrumah's own sense of frustration in his own Pan-African ventures.

Nyerere was indignant. He went public with his attack on Nkrumah. He referred to people who pretended that they were in favour of African continental union when all they cared about was to ensure that 'some stupid historian in the future' praised them for being in favour of the big continental ambition before anyone else was willing to undertake it.

Nyerere added snide remarks about 'the Redeemer' (Nkrumah's self-embraced title of the Osagyefo).

On balance, history has proved Nkrumah wrong on the question of Nyerere's commitment to liberation. Nyerere was second to none in that commitment.

At that Cairo conference of 1964 Nkrumah had asked 'What could be the result of entrusting the training of Freedom Fighters against imperialism into the hands of an imperialist agent?'

Nyerere had indeed answered 'the good Osagyefo' with sarcasm and counter-argument. But Nyerere was also already trying to sharpen his country's militancy in anti-colonial policy. At Cairo he took the posture of a leader disillusioned with the arts of persuasion in matters of liberation. He now demanded rigorous action to expel Portugal from Africa. As he put it:

'I am convinced that the finer the words the greater the harm they do to the prestige of Africa if they are not followed by action ...Africa is strong enough to drive Portugal from our Continent. Let us resolve at this conference to take the necessary action.'

Nyerere did indeed attempt to take the lead in this new militancy. He became the toughest spokesman against the British on the Rhodesian question. His country played a crucial role at the OAU Ministerial meeting at which it was decided to issue that fatal ultimatum to Britain's Prime Minister, Harold Wilson – 'Break Ian Smith or Africa will break with you.'" – (Ali A. Mazrui, "Nkrumahism and The Triple Heritage: Out of The Shadows," Third Lecture, Aggrey-Fraser-Guggisberg Memorial Lectures, University of Ghana, Legon, 2002).

Even if Nkrumah had not been overthrown, he would not have been able to send troops – all the way from Ghana to Rhodesia – to topple the white minority regime in that country. The leaders of Zambia and Tanzania would probably not have agreed to support Nkrumah's highly ambitious mission because they knew it would not have succeeded for a number of reasons.

Their armed forces at that time were weak and would not have been able to support Ghanaian troops to wage a sustained and successful military campaign against the Rhodesian army and air force.

Had the leaders of the two countries agreed to support Nkrumah's mission, their involvement in the war would have been inevitable. They would not have stood aside and let Ghanaian troops fight the war alone. They would have been forced to support them instead of just providing rear bases for them.

There were also insurmountable logistical problems. Ghanaian troops in the combat zone would have to maintain supply lines all the way to Ghana, almost 3,000 miles away from Rhodesia and Zambia, Rhodesia's neighbour which would have been the main rear base for the Ghanaian soldiers and from which they would have to launch attacks against the white-ruled territory.

Zambia would have to be prepared for a massive retaliatory response from Rhodesia's armed forces. Also, apartheid South Africa – out of kith-and-kin considerations to support fellow whites – would have entered the war to defend and protect the white minority rulers of Rhodesia, thus escalating the conflict. The South African white rulers would also have entered the war for their own security. They reasoned: If Rhodesia falls, South Africa will be the next target.

Therefore it would have been important for white-ruled South Africa to use Rhodesia as a buffer zone by helping whites in Rhodesia remain in power.

The reaction of Britain itself could not have been ignored had Nkrumah succeeded in sending Ghanaian troops to Zambia to attack Rhodesia.

The British government was not ready to allow anyone to use force in Rhodesia to remove the white minority rulers from power, ostensibly because Rhodesia was its responsibility. Yet it did nothing to justify that position.

Instead, it refused to use force to end white minority rule in Rhodesia in spite of the fact that what the white settlers had done, unilaterally declaring independence totally excluding the black majority from power, was an act of rebellion against Britain since Rhodesia was still a

144

British colony.

The Unilateral Declaration of Independence (UDI) by the white minority regime led by Prime Minister Ian Smith was clearly an act of rebellion against the Crown. As President Nyerere stated in his speech, entitled "The Honour of Africa," to the Tanzania National Assembly (parliament) on 14 December 1965 on his government's decision to break diplomatic relations with Britain, one month after Rhodesia declared independence:

"The policies of Tanzania, and of Africa, in relation to Southern Rhodesia, have always had one object, and one object only. That was, and is, to secure a rapid transition to independence on the basis of majority rule....

Africa maintains that Southern Rhodesia is at present a colony of the United Kingdom, and that ultimate responsibility for events there resides, in consequence, with the Government of the united Kingdom in London.... (But) Britain has not shown serious determination either to get rid of those in Southern Rhodesia who have usurped British power, or to replace them with representatives of the people. For it is not the independence of Rhodesia that Africa is complaining about; it is independence under a racialist minority government....

Southern Rhodesia is a British colony; its constitution is subject to the will of the British Parliament. As an international entity Southern Rhodesia does not exist. Internationally, by both law and custom, there exists only Britain and its colony.

The colony of Southern Rhodesia has been self-governing since 1923; for 43 years increasing *de facto* power has been exerted by a government based in Salisbury. But the constitution under which that government operated reserved certain powers to the British Government and Parliament in London. The fact that successive British Governments did not use their powers to prevent acts which were contrary to the interests

145

of the African people does not alter the existence of these 'Reserved Powers'; nor the ultimate responsibility of the British Government for the actions of the Southern Rhodesian government.

In saying this there is no need to argue abstract cases of law. Britain herself accepts responsibility for Southern Rhodesia. More, she claims that responsibility. Britain claims that she, and she alone, can decide what is to be done about Southern Rhodesia. The only time she has ever used her veto in the United Nations was when Ghana proposed a resolution which would have blocked the transfer to the Southern Rhodesian government of the Air Force which had been built up by the defunct Federation of Rhodesia and Nyasaland. In the Commonwealth Conferences of 1964 and 1965, the Government of Britain maintained this stand, and it was conceded by the rest of the Commonwealth - including the African members. And just over a week ago - on 6 December 1965 - Mr. Wilson, the Prime Minister of Britain, is reported to have said once again, 'Rhodesia is Britain's responsibility.'

There is thus no dispute between Britain and Africa about the British responsibility. What then of the manner in which that responsibility has been, and is being, exercised?

I do not propose to go back further than October 1964 in an examination of the British record. The record before that date is a shameful one; time after time the interests of the African majority were subjected to the selfish power hunger of the settler minority. Even after 1947, when other colonies in Africa began to feel some hope of ultimate freedom, the settlers of Southern Rhodesia were able to extend their sway. In return for some concessions on the periphery of power, some verbal acceptance of the theory of 'partnership,' they were able to secure dominance in a federation of Rhodesia with the countries, which are now Zambia and Malawi. In 1961, with the tide running hard against them, and when they were concerned to try and save their federation, they still managed to secure a constitution for Southern Rhodesia, which entrenched minority power while only appearing to make some concessions to the African population. And in 1963, at the break-up of the federation (which was established in 1953), they secured into their own hands the real instruments of power – the aeroplanes, the equipment, and the administration of the Army and the Air Force.

For the settler government of Southern Rhodesia even this was not enough. In 1963, and even more in 1964, they began to demand independence for themselves.

That was the position in October 1964....

On 27 October 1964, the Prime Minister of Britain said openly to Mr. Smith, the Prime Minister in the British colony, that a unilateral 'declaration of independence would be an open act of defiance and rebellion, and it would be treasonable to take steps to give effect to it.' These strong words meant that Africa was heartened despite the fact that the statement went on to speak only of economic consequences of such a declaration.

In November, however, the Smith government called for a referendum in support of independence for Southern Rhodesia under the 1961 constitution. He received 58,000 votes in support. I ask that this House should take particular note of that number; it is less than the total registered voters in the Dar es Salaam South constituency of Tanzania. And even that vote was only obtained after Mr. Smith had said that he was not asking for a vote in support of an illegal declaration of independence!

Threats of illegal action nonetheless continued to come from Salisbury, and apart from warnings about what would happen if they were carried out, nothing was done to those who made the threats. Indeed, by the end of the year there were indications from London that independence might be granted without majority rule. Mr. Bottomley, the British Commonwealth Secretary, was reported as saying , 'We must be satisfied that the basis on which independence is to be granted is acceptable to the people as a whole.' This ambiguous statement was clearly deliberate, and it succeeded in one of its designs. Africa thought that this was merely a tactical move, an endeavour to avoid provoking Smith before Britain was ready to deal with him....

Although UDI was declared to be an act of rebellion there was a studious avoidance by British Ministers of the statement that the rebellion would be brought down by all necessary means, including the use of force. The Smith group were never faced with that prospect. On several occasions British Ministers said, 'We shall not use force to impose a constitutional solution' to the Rhodesian situation. They never went further. Africa worried, and waited.

Even more serious for Africa was the deliberate vagueness about the ultimate objective of the negotiations (between Smith and the British government) and the opposition to UDI....

Britain's 'five principles' which had to be met before independence would be granted by the British Government did not specify the existence of majority rule. On the contrary, they clearly showed that if certain 'safeguards' were enshrined in a document, then majority rule would not be insisted upon. There was only one ambiguous statement in principle five, which many genuine people - including African leaders - believed provided a safeguard. Principle five stated that 'any basis proposed for independence must be acceptable to the people of Rhodesia as a whole.' Many of our friends said that the people of that colony could not possibly agree on an independence without majority rule, and that therefore, so long as this principle was maintained, Rhodesia would not become completely a second South Africa without hope of peaceful progress.

Tanzania was less sanguine; in the Commonwealth Conference I therefore demanded that the words *'independence on the basis of majority rule'* be included in the final communique. They were not included; and in consequence Tanzania disassociated itself from the Southern Rhodesia section of the communique. Our friends thought us needlessly suspicious. But it was quite clear to us that the British Government was willing to grant independence on the basis of minority rule.

Now it is one month after the minority government of Rhodesia has seized power.... Have we yet had the assurance (of independence on the basis of majority rule), which Tanzania sought in June? The answer is no. The 1961 constitution remains in being, with some few powers having been resumed by the Government in London. This resumption having been forced upon Britain by Smith! Let me quote Mr. Wilson, the Prime Minister of the United Kingdom, speaking in the House of Commons, London, on 23 November 1965 - 12 days after the rebellion. He said - as reported in the *Times*:

'While we have power to revoke or amend sections of the 1961 constitution we have said we have no present intention of revoking it as a whole, and I cannot at this stage foresee circumstances in which we would do so.'

Mr. Wilson went on to deal with the role of this constitution in what he calls 'the resettlement period.' He said:

'When the Governor is able to report that the people of Rhodesia are willing and able to work on constitutional paths, we are prepared to work together with their leaders to make a new start. For this purpose the 1961 constitution remains in being, though the House will realize the need for those amendments which are required to prevent its perversion and misuse such as we have seen in the last fortnight, and those amendments, too, which are needed to give effect to the five principles to which all parties in this House have subscribed'....

Later in the same speech Mr. Wilson said:

'All along we have made it plain - we did all

throughout the negotiations - that while guaranteed and unimpeded progress to majority rule is the policy of all of us, we dot believe it can be immediate.... But all of us are committed to an early attempt by the Rhodesian people to pronounce on their own future. That was the reason for the suggested referendum and for the Royal Commission.'

The thing, which I notice in the last statement, Mr. Speaker, is that this was not an assurance about majority rule; it was an assurance against majority rule.

At the end of last week the British Broadcasting Corporation (BBC) news service reported that Mr. Wilson had suggested that after all, when British authority was re-established in Southern Rhodesia, there might be a period of direct rule by the Governor with advisers from all races. As this would mean the end of the 1961 constitution I had a moment of hope; we would begin over again. But the report went on to say that Mr. Wilson stressed that majority rule could not come for a very long time - and still there was no suggestion that independence would be held up until this majority rule had finally been attained....

It is not the timing, which is causing Africa to become so angry; we could argue about time. Our anger and suspicion arise from the fact that Britain is not even now - 14 December 1965 - committed to the principle of 'independence only on the basis of majority rule.'

I must, however, now move to the question of whether Britain has shown serious determination to get rid of those in Southern Rhodesia who have usurped her power. Africa maintains that she has not....

What has Britain done since 11 November?

On that date Mr. Wilson used some strong words: he said, 'It is an illegal act, ineffective in law; an act of rebellion against the Crown and against the constitution as by law established.' But he then went on to instruct the civil servants of Southern Rhodesia to 'stay at their posts but not assist in any illegal acts.' He was unable to explain how they could do that when they were serving an illegal government.

As regards the use of force Mr. Wilson repeated his stock phrase despite the changed circumstances. Britain would not use force to impose a constitutional settlement he said, but he went on to say that the British Government 'would give full consideration to any appeal from the Governor for help to restore law and order.' Mr. Wilson refrained from explaining how the law could be more broken than it had been by the usurpation of power, that is to say, by treason. He refrained later from explaining how the Governor was to transmit his appeal once the telephone had been taken from him as well as all the furniture of his office, his staff and his transport.

Instead, Mr. Wilson obtained the approval of the British Parliament for economic action against the regime. Capital exports to southern Rhodesia were stopped; exchange restrictions were imposed; Commonwealth preference was suspended, and a ban was imposed on the British import of Rhodesian tobacco and sugar. The British Foreign Secretary was sent to the United Nations to secure international support for these actions.

The United Nations was highly critical: it demanded further action. Finally, on 20 November Britain accepted a Security Council resolution which included this phrase: 'Calls upon all states...to do their utmost in order to break all economic relations with Southern Rhodesia, including an embargo on oil and petroleum products'....

On 23 November Mr. Wilson spoke to the House of Commons, saying, 'We are going to study all aspects of trade and oil.... We are not going in for a trade embargo or oil embargo alone.' And in explanation of this, he said that there are many difficulties and 'there is the position of Zambia to be considered'! That Zambia had supported the resolution appeared irrelevant to the British Prime Minister, who clearly thought he knew the business of that independent African state better than President Kaunda. On 1 December Mr. Wilson again said, 'We are not contemplating an embargo immediately.'

What is Africa expected to think of this mockery of a UN resolution which was already - at Britain's insistence - less than a firm, binding declaration of determination to defeat Smith?

On 1 December, however, Mr. Wilson announced new and much sterner economic measures against Rhodesia. Ninety-five per cent of Rhodesia's exports to Britain were then blocked, and financial measures taken which could have had a fairly quick and fairly severe effect on the economy of that colony. But Mr. Smith of Rhodesia was yesterday reported to have said that these have come too late to affect Rhodesia's economy. I do not believe that he is bluffing. He has had weeks in which to prepare for these measures. But the timing is not my only criticism. I have argued that economic sanctions against Rhodesia will not work as long as South Africa is allowed to trade freely with the rebel colony. And it is Britain, which has blocked obligatory sanctions under Chapter 7 of the UN Charter....

The British Government has not shown serious determination either to get rid of those in Southern Rhodesia who have usurped British power, or to replace them with representatives of the people.... Britain... has failed to live up to the responsibilities she has claimed, and she has failed to protect...an independent state (Zambia) which is threatened because of her failure to immediately overthrow the rebel regime." – (Julius K. Nyerere, "The Honour of Africa," in J.K. Nyerere, *Freedom and Socialism: A Selection from Writings and Speeches 1965 - 1967* (Dar es Salaam, Tanzania: Oxford University Press, 1968), pp. 115 - 133; *The Nationalist*, Dar es salaam, Tanzania, December 15, 1968; *Standard*, Dar es Salaam, Tanzania, December 15, 1968.

The Rhodesian crisis was the biggest challenge the newly independent African countries faced collectively in the mid-sixties. There was the Congo crisis before that, starting in 1960. But that was before many countries on the continent won independence.

The two crises also provided a theatre in which some of the continent's most prominent leaders, Nkrumah and Nyerere, played a very important role to secure African interests.

Nkrumah sent Ghanaian troops to Congo as an integral part of the UN peacekeeping mission to restore peace and maintain the country's territorial integrity threatened by the secession of Katanga Province and other secessionist attempts including one in South Kasai Province. He demonstrated that African countries can play a role to restore and maintain peace on their continent in spite of their weakness. It was a weakness he felt could be overcome if the countries collectively established an African High Command to defend the continent. It was during the Congo crisis that he proposed formation of such a continental force.

In the case of the Rhodesian crisis, it was Nyerere, among all the leaders in independent Africa, who emerged as the toughest spokesman and one of the strongest supporters of the liberation movements in Rhodesia and other countries of southern Africa still under white minority rule.

The Rhodesian crisis, triggered by the unilateral declaration of independence (UDI) by the white minority rulers of Rhodesia, coincided with Nkrumah's downfall in a military coup orchestrated by the United States and supported by Britain, France and West Germany.

He was overthrown two-and-a-half months after Rhodesia declared independence, marking the end of a political career of one of the most dynamic leaders in the history of post-colonial Africa.

Nkrumah and Nyerere embodied the true spirit of Pan-Africanism in an era when being African meant being African. Unfortunately, the spirit they embodied died with them.

Appendix I:

Nkrumah's speech to the first conference of the Organisation of African Unity (OAU) when the OAU was formed in Addis Ababa, Ethiopia, 25 May 1963. His book, *Africa Must Unite*, was also published in May 1963 to coincide with the formation of the OAU as an attempt to encourage his fellow leaders to agree with his plan for immediate continental unification under one government.

Your Excellences, Colleagues, Brothers and Friends,

At the first gathering of African Heads of State, to which I had the honour of playing host, there were representatives of eight independent States only. Today, five years later, we meet as the representatives of no less than thirty-two States, the guests of His Imperial Majesty, Haile Selassie, the First, and the Government and people of Ethiopia. To His Imperial Majesty, I wish to express, on behalf of the Government and people of Ghana my deep appreciation for a most cordial welcome and generous hospitality.

The increase in our number in this short space of time is open testimony to the indomitable and irresistible surge of our peoples for independence. It is also a token of the revolutionary speed of world events in the latter half of this century. In the task which is before us of unifying our continent we must fall in with that pace or be left behind. The task cannot be attached in the tempo of any other age than our own. To fall behind the unprecedented momentum of actions and events in our time will be to court failure and our own undoing.

A whole continent has imposed a mandate upon us to lay the foundation of our Union at this Conference. It is our responsibility to execute this mandate by creating here and now the formula upon which the requisite superstructure may be erected.

On this continent it has not taken us long to discover that the struggle against colonialism does not end with the attainment of national independence. Independence is only the prelude to a new and more involved struggle for the right to conduct our own economic and social affairs; to construct our society according to our aspirations, unhampered by crushing and humiliating neo-colonialist controls and interference.

From the start we have been threatened with frustration where rapid change is imperative and with instability where sustained effort and ordered rule are indispensable.

No sporadic act nor pious resolution can resolve our present problems. Nothing will be of avail, except the united act of a united Africa. We have already reached, the stage where we must unite or sink into that condition which has made Latin America the unwilling and distressed prey of imperialism after one and a half centuries of political independence.

As a continent we have emerged into independence in a different age, with imperialism grown stronger, more ruthless and experienced, and more dangerous in its international associations. Our economic advancement demands the end of colonialist and neo-colonialist domination in Africa.

But just as we understood that the shaping of our national destinies required of each of us our political independence and bent all our strength to this attainment, so we must recognise that our economic independence resides in our African union and requires the same concentration upon the political achievement.

The unity of our continent, no less than our separate independence, will be delayed if, indeed, we do not lose it, by hobnobbing with colonialism. African Unity is, above all, a political kingdom which can only be gained by political means. The social and economic development of Africa will come only within the political kingdom, not the other way around. The United States of America, the Union of Soviet Socialist Republics, were the political decisions of revolutionary peoples before they became mighty realities of social power and material wealth.

How, except by our united efforts, will the richest and still enslaved parts of our continent be freed from colonial occupation and become available to us for the total development of our continent? Every step in the decolonisation of our continent has brought greater resistance in those areas where colonial garrisons are available to colonialism.

This is the great design of the imperialist interests that buttress colonialism and neo-colonialism, and we would be deceiving ourselves in the most cruel way were we to regard their individual actions as separate and unrelated. When Portugal violates Senegal's border, when Verwoed allocated one-seventh of South Africa's budget to military and police, when France builds as part of her defence policy an interventionist force that can intervene, more especially in French-speaking Africa, when Welensky talks of Southern Rhodesia joining South Africa, it is all part of a carefully calculated pattern working towards a single end: the continued enslavement of our still dependent brothers and an onslaught upon the independence of our sovereign African States.

Do we have any other weapon against this design but our unity? Is not our unity essential to guard our own freedom as well as to win freedom for our oppressed brothers, the Freedom Fighters?

Is it not unity alone that can weld us into an effective force, capable of creating our own progress and making our valuable contribution to world peace? Which independent African State will claim that its financial structure and banking institutions are fully harnessed to its national development? Which will claim that its material resources and human energies are available for its own national aspirations? Which will disclaim a substantial measure of disappointment and disillusionment in its agricultural and urban development?

In independent Africa we are already re-experiencing the instability and frustration which existed under colonial rule. We are fast learning that political independence is not enough to rid us of the consequences of colonial rule.

The movement of the masses of the people of Africa for freedom from that kind of rule was not only a revolt against the conditions which it imposed.

Our people supported us in our fight for independence because they believed that African Governments could cure the ills of the past in a way which could never be accomplished under colonial rule. If, therefore, now that we are independent we allow the same conditions to exist that existed in colonial days, all the resentment which overthrew colonialism will be mobilised against us.

The resources are there. It is for us to marshal them in the active service of our people. Unless we do this by our concerted efforts, within the framework of our combined planning, we shall not progress at the tempo demanded by today's events and the mood of our people. The symptoms of our troubles will grow, and the troubles themselves become chronic. It will then be too late even for Pan-African Unity to secure for us stability and tranquillity in our labours for a continent of social justice and material well-being. Unless we establish African Unity now, we who are sitting here today shall tomorrow be the victims and martyrs of neo-colonialism.

There is evidence on every side that the imperialists have not withdrawn from our affairs. There are times, as in the Congo, when their interference is manifest. But generally it is covered up under the clothing of many agencies, which meddle in our domestic affairs, to foment dissension within our borders and to create an atmosphere of tension and political instability. As long as we do not do away with the root causes of discontent, we lend aid to these neo-colonialist forces, and shall become our own executioners. We cannot ignore the teachings of history.

Our continent is probably the richest in the world for minerals and industrial and agricultural primary materials. From the Congo alone, Western firms exported copper, rubber, cotton, and other goods to the value of 2, 773 billion dollars in the ten years between 1945 and 1955, and from South Africa, Western gold mining companies have drawn a profit, in the four years, between 1947 to 1951, of 814 billion dollars.

Our continent certainly exceeds all the others in potential hydroelectric power, which some experts assess as 42 per cent of the world's total. What need is there for us to remain hewers for the industrialised areas of the world?

It is said, of course, that we have no capital, no industrial skill, no communications and no internal markets, and that we cannot even agree among ourselves how best to utilise our resources.

Yet all the stock exchanges in the world are preoccupied with Africa's gold, diamonds, uranium, platinum, copper and iron ores. Our capital flows out in streams to irrigate the whole system of Western economy. Fifty-two per cent of the gold in Fort Knox at this moment, where the U. S. A. stores its bullion, is believed to have originated from our shores. Africa provides more than 60 per cent of the world's gold. A great deal of the uranium for nuclear power, of copper for electronics, of titanium for supersonic projectiles, of iron and steel for heavy industries, of other minerals and raw materials for lighter industries – the basic economic might of the foreign Powers – come from our continent.

Experts have estimated that the Congo basin alone can produce enough food crops to satisfy the requirements of nearly half the population of the whole world.

For centuries Africa has been the milk cow of the Western world. It was our continent that helped the Western world to build up its accumulated wealth.

It is true that we are now throwing off the yoke of colonialism as fast as we can, but our success in this direction is equally matched by an intense effort on the part of imperialism to continue the exploitation of our resources by creating divisions among us.

When the colonies of the American Continent sought to free themselves from imperialism in the 18th century there was no threat of neo-colonialism in the sense in which we know it today. The American States were therefore free to form and fashion the unity which was best suited to their needs and to frame a constitution to hold their unity together without any form of interference from external sources. We, however, are having to grapple with outside interventions. How much more, then do we need to come together in the African unity that alone can save us from the clutches of neo-colonialism.

We have the resources. It was colonialism in the first place that prevented us from accumulating the effective capital; but we ourselves have failed to make full use of our power in independence to mobilise our resources for the most effective take-off into thorough going economic and social development. We have been too busy nursing our separate States to understand fully the basic need of our union, rooted in common purpose, common planning and common endeavour. A union that ignores these fundamental necessities will be but a shame. It is only by uniting our productive capacity and the resultant production that we can amass capital. And once we start, the momentum will increase.

With capital controlled by our own banks, harnessed to our own true industrial and agricultural development, we shall make our advance. We shall accumulate machinery and establish steel works, iron foundries and factories; we shall link the various States of our continent with communications; we shall astound the world with our hydroelectric power; we shall drain marshes and swamps, clear infested areas, feed the under-nourished, and rid our people of parasites and disease. It is within the possibility of science and technology to make even the Sahara bloom into a vast field with verdant vegetation for agricultural and industrial developments. We shall harness the radio, television, giant printing presses to lift our people from the dark recesses of illiteracy.

A decade ago, these would have been visionary words, the fantasies of an idle dreamer. But this is the age in which science has transcended the limits of the material world, and technology has invaded the silences of nature. Time and space have been reduced to unimportant abstractions. Giant machines make roads, clear forests, dig dams, layout aerodromes; monster trucks and planes distribute goods; huge laboratories manufacture drugs; complicated geological surveys are made; mighty power stations are built; colossal factories erected – all at an incredible speed. The world is no longer moving through bush paths or on camels and donkeys.

We cannot afford to pace our needs, our development, our security to the gait of camels and donkeys. We cannot afford not to cut down the overgrown bush of outmoded attitudes that obstruct our path to the modern open road of the widest and earliest achievement of economic independence and the raising up of the lives of our people to the highest level.

Even for other continents lacking tile resources of Africa, this is the age that sees the end of human want. For us it is a simple matter of grasping with certainty our heritage by using the political might of unity. All we need to do is to develop with our united strength the enormous resources of our continent. A United Africa will provide a stable field of foreign investment, which will encourage as long as it does not behave inimically to our African interests. For such investment would add by its enterprises to the development of the national economy, employment and training of our people, and will be welcome to Africa. In dealing with a united Africa, investors will no longer have to weigh with concern the risks of negotiating with governments in one period which may not exist in the very next period. Instead of dealing or negotiating with so many separate States at a time they will be dealing with one united government pursuing a harmonized continental policy.

What is the alternative to this? If we falter at this stage, and let time pass for neo-colonialism to consolidate its position on this continent, what will be the fate of our people who have put their trust in us? What will be the fate of our freedom fighters? What will be the fate of other African Territories that are not yet free?

Unless we can establish great industrial complexes in Africa – which we can only do in united Africa – we must have our peasantry to the mercy of foreign cash crop markets, and face the same unrest which overthrew the colonialists? What use to the farmer is education and mechanisation, what use is even capital for development;

161

unless we can ensure for him and a fair price and ready market? What has the peasant, worker and farmer gained from political independence, unless we can ensure for him a fair return for his labour and a higher standard of living?

Unless we can establish great industrial complexes in Africa, what have the urban worker, and all those peasants on overcrowded land gained from political independence? If they are to remain unemployed or in unskilled occupation, what will avail them the better facilities for education, technical training, energy and ambition which independence enables us to provide?

There is hardly any African State without frontier problems with its adjacent neighbours. It would be futile for me to enumerate them because they are already familiar to us all. But let me suggest to Your Excellences, that this fatal relic of colonialism will drive us to war against one another as our unplanned and uncoordinated industrial development expands, just as happened in Europe.

Unless we succeed in arresting the danger through mutual understanding on fundamental issues and through African Unity, which will render existing boundaries obsolete and superfluous, we shall have fought in vain for independence. Only African Unity can heal this festering sore of boundary disputes between our various States. Your Excellences, the remedy for these ills is ready to our hand. It stares us in the face at every customs barrier, it shouts to us from every African heart. By creating a true political union of all the independent States of Africa, we can tackle hopefully every emergency, every enemy and every
complexity. This is not because we are a race of superman, but because we have emerged in the age of science and technology in which poverty, ignorance and disease are no longer the masters, but the retreating foes of mankind. We have emerged in the age of socialized planning, when production and distribution are not governed by chaos,

greed and self-interest, but by social needs. Together with the rest of mankind, we have awakened from Utopian dreams to pursue practical blueprints for progress and social justice.

Above all, we have emerged at a time when a continental land mass like Africa with its population approaching three hundred million are necessary to the economic capitalization and profitability of modern productive methods and techniques. Not one of us working singly and individually can successfully attain the fullest development. Certainly, in the circumstances, it will not be possible to give adequate assistance to sister States trying, against the most difficult conditions, to improve their economic and social structures. Only a united Africa functioning under a Union Government can forcefully mobilize the material and moral resources of our separate countries and apply them efficiently and energetically to bring a rapid change in the conditions of our people.

If we do not approach the problems in Africa with a common front and a common purpose, we shall be haggling and wrangling among ourselves until we are colonized again and become the tolls of a far greater colonialism than we suffered hitherto.

Unite we must. Without necessarily sacrificing our sovereignties, big or small, we can, here and now, forge a political union based on Defence, Foreign Affairs and Diplomacy, and a common Citizenship, an African currency, an African Monetary Zone and an African Central Bank. We must unite in order to achieve the full liberation of our continent. We need a common Defence system with an African High Command to ensure the stability and security of Africa.

We have been charged with this sacred task by our own people, and we cannot betray their trust by failing them. We will be mocking the hopes of our people if we show the slightest hesitation or delay by tackling realistically this question of African Unity.

163

The supply of arms or other military aid to the colonial oppressors in Africa must be regarded not only as aid in the vanquishment of the freedom fighters battling for their African independence, but as an act of aggression against the whole of Africa. How can we meet this aggression except by the full weight of our united strength?

Many of us have made non-alignment an article of faith on this continent. We have no wish, and no intention of being drawn into the Cold War. But with the present weakness and insecurity of our States in the context of world politics, the search for bases and spheres of influence brings the Cold War into Africa with its danger of nuclear warfare. Africa should be declared a nuclear-free zone and freed from cold war exigencies. But we cannot make this demand mandatory unless we support it from a position of strength to be found only in our unity.

Instead, many Independent African States are involved by military pacts with the former colonial powers. The stability and security which such devices seek to establish are illusory, for the metropolitan Powers seize the opportunity to support their neo-colonialist controls by direct military involvement. We have seen how the neo-colonialists use their bases to entrench themselves and attack neighbouring independent States. Such bases are centers of tension and potential danger spots of military conflict. They threaten the security not only of the country in which they are situated but of neighbouring countries as well. How can we hope to make Africa a nuclear-free zone and independent of cold war pressure with such military involvement on our continent? Only by counter-balancing a common defence force with a common defence policy based upon our desire for an Africa untrammelled by foreign dictation or military and nuclear presence. This will require an all-embracing African High Command, especially if the military pacts with the imperialists are to be renounced. It is the only way we can break these direct links between the colonialism of the past and the neo-colonialism which disrupts us today.

We do not want nor do we visualize an African High Command in the terms of the power politics that now rule a great part of the world, but as an essential and indispensable instrument for ensuring stability and security in Africa.

We need a unified economic planning for Africa. Until the economic power of Africa is in our hands, the masses can have no real concern and no real interest for safeguarding our security, for ensuring the stability of our regimes, and for bending their strength to the fulfilment of our ends. With our united resources, energies and talents we have the means, as soon as we show the will, to transform the economic structures of our individual States from poverty to that of wealth, from, inequality to the satisfaction of popular needs. Only on a continental basis shall we be able to plan the proper utilisation of all our resources for the full development of our continent.

How else will we retain our own capital for our development? How else will we establish an internal market for our own industries? By belonging to different economic zones, how will we break down the currency and trading barriers between African States, and how will the economically stronger amongst us be able to assist the weaker and less developed States?

It is important to remember that independent financing and independent development cannot take place without an independent currency. A currency system that is backed by the resources of a foreign State is *ipso facto* subject to the trade and financial arrangements of that foreign country.

Because we have so many customs and currency barriers as a result of being subject to the different currency systems of foreign powers, this has served to widen the gap between us in Africa. How, for example, can related communities and families trade with, and support one another successfully, if they find themselves divided by national boundaries and currency restrictions? The only alternative open to them in these circumstances, is to use smuggled currency and enrich national and international racketeers and crooks who prey upon our financial and economic difficulties.

No independent African State today by itself has a chance to follow an independent course of economic development, and many of us who have tried to do this have been almost ruined or have had to return to the fold of the former colonial rulers. This position will not change unless we have unified policy working at the continental level. The first step towards our cohesive economy would be a unified monetary zone, with, initially, an agreed common parity for our currencies. To facilitate this arrangement, Ghana would change to a decimal system. When we find that the arrangement of a fixed common parity is working successfully, there would seem to be no reason for not instituting one common currency and a single bank of issue. With a common currency from one common bank of issue we should be able to stand erect on our own feet because such an arrangement would be fully backed by the combined national products of the States composing the union. After all, the purchasing power of money depends on productivity and the productive exploitation of the natural, human and physical resources of the nation.

While we are assuring our stability by a common defence system, and our economy is being orientated beyond foreign control by a Common currency, Monetary Zone and Central Bank of Issue, we can investigate the resources of our continent. We can begin to ascertain whether in reality we are the richest, and not, as we have been taught to believe, the poorest among the continents. We can determine whether we possess the largest potential in hydroelectric power, and whether we can harness it and other sources of energy to our own industries. We can proceed to plan our industrialization on a continental scale, and to build up a common market for nearly three hundred million people.

Common Continental Planning for the Industrial and Agricultural development of Africa is a vital necessity.

So many blessings must flow from our unity; so many disasters must follow on our continued disunity, that our failure to unite today will not be attributed by posterity only to faulty reasoning and lack of courage, but to our capitulation before the forces of imperialism.

The hour of history which has brought us to this assembly is a revolutionary hour. It is the hour of decision. For the first time, the economic imperialism which menaces us is itself challenged by the irresistible will of our people.

The masses of the people of Africa are crying for unity. The people of Africa call for a breaking down of boundaries that keep them apart. They demand an end to the border disputes between sister African States – disputes that arise out of the artificial barriers that divided us. It was colonialism's purpose that left us with our border irredentism that rejected our ethnic and cultural fusion.

Our people call for unity so that they may not lose their patrimony in the perpetual service of neo-colonialism. In their fervent push for unity, they understand that only its realization will give full meaning to their freedom and our African independence.

It is this popular determination that must move us on to a Union of Independent African States. In delay lies danger to our well-being, to tour very existence as free States. It has been suggested that our approach of unity should be gradual, that it should go piece-meal. This point of view conceives of Africa as a static entity with "frozen" problems which can be eliminated one by one and when all have been cleared then we can come together and say: "Now all is well. Let us unite." This view takes no account of the impact of external pressures. Nor does it take cognizance of the danger that delay can deepen our isolations and exclusiveness; that it can enlarge our differences and set us drifting further and further apart into the net of neo-colonialism, so that our union will become nothing but a fading hope, and the great design of Africa's full redemption will be lost, perhaps, forever.

The view is also expressed that our difficulties could be resolved simply by a greater collaboration through cooperative association in our inter-territorial relationships. This way of looking at our problems denies a proper conception of their inter-relationship and mutuality. It denies faith in a future for African advancement, in African independence. It betrays a sense of solution only in continued reliance upon external sources through bilateral agreements for economic and other forms of aid.

The fact is that although we have been cooperating and associating with one another in various fields of common endeavour even before colonial times, this has not given us the continental identity and the political and economic force which would help us to deal effectively with the complicated problems confronting us in Africa today. As far as foreign aid is concerned, a United Africa would be in a more favourable position to attract assistance from foreign sources. There is the far more compelling advantage which this arrangement offers, in that aid will come from anywhere to Africa because our bargaining power would become infinitely greater. We shall no longer be dependent upon aid from restricted sources. We shall have the world to choose from.

What are we looking for in Africa? Are we looking for Charters, conceived in the light of the United Nations example? A type of United Nations organisation whose decisions are framed on the basis of resolutions that in our experience have sometimes been ignored by member States? Where groupings are formed and pressures develop in accordance with the interest of the group concerned? Or is it intended that Africa should be turned into a lose organization of States on the model of the organization of the American States, in which the weaker States within it can be at the mercy of the stronger or more powerful ones politically or economically or at the mercy of some powerful outside nations or group of nations? Is this the kind of association we want for ourselves in the United Africa we all speak of with such feeling and emotion?

Your Excellences, permit me to ask: is this the kind of framework we desire for our United Africa? And arrangement which in future could permit Ghana or Nigeria or the Sudan, or Liberia, or Egypt or Ethiopia for example, to use pressure, which either superior economic or political influence gives, to dictate the flow and the direction of trade from, say, Burundi or Togo or Nyasaland to Mozambique?

We all want a United Africa, united not only in our concept of what unity can connotes, but united in our common desire to move forward together and dealing with all the problems that can best be solved only on a continental basis.

When the first Congress of the United States met many years ago at Philadelphia, one of the delegates sounded the first chore of unity by declaring that they had met in a "state of nature" in other words, they were not at Philadelphia as Virginians, or Pennsylvanians, but simply as Americans. This reference to themselves as Americans was in those days a new and strange experience. May I dare to assert equally on this occasion, Your Excellences that we meet here today not as Ghanaians, Guineans, Egyptians, Algerians, Moroccans, Malians, Liberians, Congolese or Nigerians but as Africans. Africans united in our resolve to remain here until we have agreed on the basic principles of a new compact of unity among ourselves which guaranties for us and future a new arrangement of continental government.

If we succeed in establishing a new set of principles as the basis of a new Charter or Statute for the establishment of a Continental Unity of Africa and the creation of social and political progress for our people then, in my view, this Conference should mark the end of our various groupings and regional blocs. But if we fail and let this grand and historic opportunity slip by then we should give way to greater dissension and division among us for which the people of Africa will never forgive us. And the popular and progressive forces and movements within Africa will condemn us. I am sure therefore that we should not fail them.

I have spoken at some length, Your Excellences, because it is necessary for us all to explain not only to one another present here but also to our people who have entrusted to us the fate and destiny of Africa. We must therefore not leave this place until we have set up effective machinery for achieving African Unity. To this end, I now propose for your consideration the following:

As a first step, Your Excellences, a Declaration of Principles uniting and binding us together and to which we must all faithfully and loyally adhere, and laying the foundations of unity should be set down. And there should also be a formal declaration that all the Independent African States here and now agree to the establishment of a Union of African States.

As a second and urgent step for the realization of the unification of Africa, an All-Africa Committee of Foreign Ministers be set up now, and that before we rise from this Conference a day should be fixed for them to meet.

This Committee should establish on behalf of the Heads of our Governments, a permanent body of officials and experts to work out a machinery for the Union Government of Africa. This body of officials and experts should be made up of two of the brains from each Independent African State. The various Charters of the existing groupings and other relevant document could also be submitted to the officials and experts. A praesidium consisting of the Head of the Governments of the Independent African States should be call upon to meet and adopt a Constitution and others recommendations that will launch the Union Government of Africa.

We must also decide on allocation where this body of officials and experts will work as the new Headquarters or Capital of our Union Government. Some central place in Africa might be the fairest suggestion either at Bangui in the Central African Republic or Leopoldville in Congo. My colleagues may have other proposals. The Committee of Foreign Ministers, officials and experts should be empowered to establish:

1. A Commission to frame a Constitution for a Union Government of African States;

2. A Commission to work out a continent-wide plan for a unified or common economic and industrial programme for Africa; this plan should include proposals for setting up:

A Common Market for Africa

An African currency

African Monetary Zone

African Central Bank, and

Continental Communications System;

3. A Commission to draw up details for a Common Foreign Policy and Diplomacy;

4. A Commission to produce plans for a Common System of Defence;

5. A Commission to make proposals for Common African Citizenship.

These Commissions will report to the Committee of Foreign Ministers who should in turn submit within six months of this Conference their recommendations to the

Praesidium. The Praesidium meeting in Conference at the Union Headquarters will consider and approve the recommendations of the Committee of Foreign Ministers.

In order to provide funds immediately for the work of the permanent officials and experts of the Headquarters of the Union, I suggest that a special Committed be set up now to work a budget for this.

Your Excellences, with these steps, I submit, we shall be irrevocably committed to the road which will bring us to a Union Government of Africa. Only a united Africa with central political direction can successfully give effective material and moral support to our Freedom Fighters in Southern Rhodesia, Angola, Mozambique, South-West Africa, Bechuanaland, Swaziland, Basutoland, Portuguese Guinea, etc., and of course South Africa.

Appendix II

Speech by Julius Nyerere on Ghana's 40th independence anniversary in Accra

In May 1963, 32 independent African states met in Addis Ababa, founded the Organisation of African Unity (OAU), and established the Liberation Committee of the new organisation, charging it with the duty of coordinating the liberation struggle in those parts of Africa still under colonial rule. The following year, 1964, the OAU met in Cairo [Egypt]. The Cairo Summit is remembered mainly for the declaration of the heads of state of independent Africa to respect the borders inherited from colonialism. The principle of non-interference in internal affairs of member states of the OAU had been enshrined in the [OAU] Charter itself. Respect for the borders inherited from colonialism came from the Cairo Declaration of 1964.

In 1965, the OAU met in Accra [Ghana]. That summit is not as well remembered as the founding summit in 1963 or the Cairo Summit of 1964. The fact that Nkrumah did not last long as head of state of Ghana after that summit may have contributed to the comparative obscurity of that important summit. But I want to suggest that the reason

173

why we do not talk much about [the 1965] summit is probably psychological: it was a failure. That failure still haunts us today.

The founding fathers of the OAU had set themselves two major objectives: the total liberation of our continent from colonialism and settler minorities, and the unity of Africa. The first objective was expressed through the immediate establishment of the Liberation Committee by the founding summit [of 1963]. The second objective was expressed in the name of the organisation – the Organisation of African Unity.

Critics could say that the [OAU] Charter itself, with its great emphasis on the sovereign independence of each member state, combined with the Cairo Declaration on the sanctity of the inherited borders, make it look like the "Organisation of African Disunity". But that would be carrying criticism too far and ignoring the objective reasons which led to the principles of non-interference in the Cairo Declaration. What the founding fathers – certainly a hardcore of them – had in mind was a genuine desire to move Africa towards greater unity. We loathed the balkanisation of the continent into small unviable states, most of which had borders which did not make ethnic or geographical sense.

The Cairo Declaration was promoted by a profound realisation of the absurdity of those borders. It was quite clear that some adventurers would try to change those borders by force of arms. Indeed, it was already happening. Ethiopia and Somalia were at war over inherited borders.

Nkrumah was opposed to balkanisation as much as he was opposed to colonialism in Africa. To him and to a number of us, the two – balkanisation and colonialism – were twins. Genuine liberation of Africa had to attack both twins. A struggle against colonialism must go hand in hand with a struggle against the balkanisation of Africa.

Kwame Nkrumah was the great crusader of African

unity. He wanted the Accra Summit of 1965 to establish a union government for the whole of independent Africa. But we failed. The one minor reason is that Kwame, like all great believers, underestimated the degree of suspicion and animosity which his crusading passion had created among a substantial number of his fellow heads of state. The major reason was linked to the first: already too many of us had a vested interest in keeping Africa divided.

East Africa

Prior to the independence of Tanganyika, I had been advocating that East African countries should federate and then achieve independence as a single political unit. I had said publicly that I was willing to delay Tanganyika's independence in order to enable all the three mainland countries to achieve their independence together as a single federated state. I made the suggestion because of my fear – proved correct by later events – that it would be very difficult to unite our countries if we let them achieve independence separately.

Once you multiply national anthems, national flags and national passports, seats of the United Nations, and individuals entitled to a 21-gun salute, not to speak of a host of ministers, prime ministers and envoys, you would have a whole army of powerful people with vested interests in keeping Africa balkanised. That was what Nkrumah encountered in 1965. After the failure to establish the union government at the Accra Summit, I heard one head of state express with relief that he was happy to be returning home to his country still head of state. To this day, I cannot tell whether he was serious or joking.

But he may well have been serious, because Kwame Nkrumah was very serious and the fear of a number of us of losing our precious status was quite palpable. But I never believed that the 1965 Accra Summit would have established a union government for Africa. When I say that we failed, that is not what I mean; for that clearly was an unrealistic objective for a single summit.

What I mean is that we did not even discuss a mechanism for pursuing the objective of a politically united Africa. We had a Liberation Committee already. We should have at least had a Unity Committee or undertaken to establish one. We did not. And after Kwame Nkrumah was removed from the African scene, nobody took up the challenge again.

Confession and plea

So my remaining remarks have a confession and a plea. The confession is that we of the first generation leaders of independent Africa have not pursued the objective of African unity with vigour, commitment and [the] sincerity that it deserved. Yet that does not mean that unity is now irrelevant. Does the experience of the last three or four decades of Africa's independence dispel the need for African unity?

With our success in the liberation struggle, Africa today has 53 independent states, 21 more than those which met in Addis Ababa in May 1963. [With South Sudan's independence in 2011, Africa now has 54 independent states.] If numbers were horses, Africa today would be riding high! Africa would be the strongest continent in the world, for it occupies more seats in the UN General Assembly than any other continent.

Yet the reality is that ours is the poorest and weakest continent in the world. And our weakness is pathetic. Unity will not end our weakness, but until we unite, we cannot even begin to end that weakness. So this is my plea to the new generation of African leaders and African peoples: work for unity with the firm conviction that without unity, there is no future for Africa. That is, of course, assuming that we still want to have a place under the sun.

I reject the glorification of the nationstate [that] we inherited from colonialism, and the artificial nations we are trying to forge from that inheritance. We are all Africans trying very hard to be Ghanaians or Tanzanians. Fortunately for Africa, we have not been completely successful.

The outside world hardly recognises our Ghanaianness or Tanzanian-ness. What the outside world recognises about us is our Africanness. Hitler was a German, Mussolini was an Italian, Franco was a Spaniard, Salazar was Portuguese, Stalin was a Russian or a Georgian. Nobody expected Churchill to be ashamed of Hitler. He was probably ashamed of Chamberlain. Nobody expected Charles de Gaulle to be ashamed of Hitler, he was probably ashamed of the complicity of Vichy. It is the Germans and Italians and Spaniards and Portuguese who feel uneasy about those dictators in their respective countries.

Not so in Africa. Idi Amin was in Uganda but of Africa. Jean Bokassa was in Central Africa but of Africa. Some of the dictators are still alive in their respective countries, but they are all of Africa. They are all Africans, and all perceived by the outside world as Africans.

When I travel outside Africa, the description of me as a former president of Tanzania is a fleeting affair. It does not stick. Apart from the ignorant who sometimes asked me whether Tanzania was in Johannesburg, even to those who knew better, what stuck in the minds of my hosts was the fact of my African-ness.

So I had to answer questions about the atrocities of the Amins and Bokassas of Africa. Mrs [Indira] Ghandi [the former Indian prime minister] did not have to answer questions about the atrocities of the Marcoses of Asia. Nor does Fidel Castro have to answer questions about the atrocities of the Somozas of Latin America.

But when I travel or meet foreigners, I have to answer questions about Somalia, Liberia, Rwanda, Burundi and Zaire, as in the past I used to answer questions about Mozambique, Angola, Zimbabwe, Namibia or South Africa.

And the way I was perceived is the way most of my fellow heads of state were perceived. And that is the way you [the people of Africa] are all being perceived. So accepting the fact that we are Africans, gives you a much more worthwhile challenge than the current desperate attempts to fossilise Africa into the wounds inflicted upon it by the vultures of imperialism. Do not be proud of your shame. Reject the return to the tribe, there is richness of culture out there which we must do everything we can to preserve and share.

But it is utter madness to think that if these artificial, unviable states which we are trying to create are broken up into tribal components and we turn those into nation-states we might save ourselves. That kind of political and social atavism spells catastrophe for Africa. It would be the end of any kind of genuine development for Africa. It would fossilise Africa into a worse state than the one in which we are.

The future

The future of Africa, the modernisation of Africa that has a place in the 21st century, is linked with its decolonisation and detribalisation. Tribal atavism would be giving up any hope for Africa. And of all the sins that Africa can commit, the sin of despair would be the most unforgivable.

Reject the nonsense of dividing the African peoples into Anglophones, Francophones, and Lusophones. This attempt to divide our peoples according to the language of their former colonial masters must be rejected with the firmness and utter contempt that it richly deserves.

178

The natural owners of those wonderful languages are busy building a united Europe. But Europe is strong even without unity. Europe has less need of unity, and the strength that comes from unity, than Africa.

A new generation of self-respecting Africans should spit in the face of anybody who suggests that our continent should remain divided and fossilised in the shame of colonialism, in order to satisfy the national pride of our former colonial masters. Africa must unite! That was the title of one of Kwame Nkrumah's books. That call is more urgent today than ever before.

Together, we, the peoples of Africa will be incomparably stronger internationally than we are now with our multiplicity of unviable states. The needs of our separate countries can be, and are being, ignored by the rich and powerful. The result is that Africa is marginalised when international decisions affecting our vital interests are made. Unity will not make us rich, but it can make it difficult for Africa and the African peoples to be disregarded and humiliated. And it will, therefore, increase the effectiveness of the decisions we make and try to implement for our development.

My generation led Africa to political freedom. The current generation of leaders and peoples of Africa must pick up the flickering torch of African freedom, refuel it with their enthusiasm and determination, and carry it forward.

Nyerere and Nkrumah in 1963

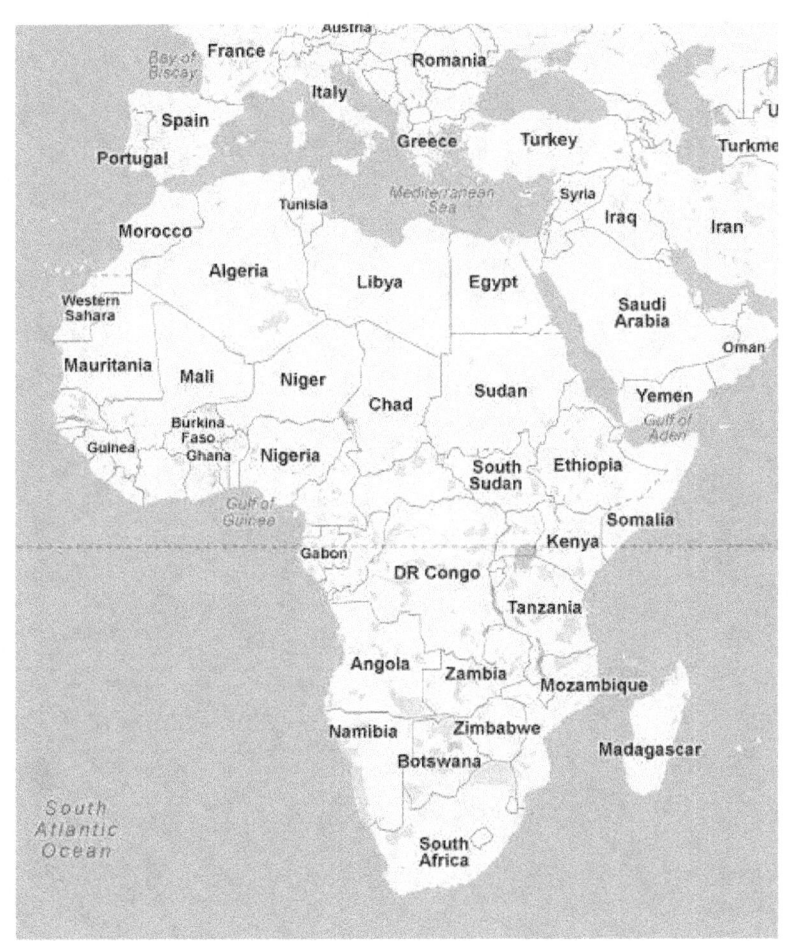

www.ingramcontent.com/pod-product-compliance
Lightning Source LLC
Chambersburg PA
CBHW060623290526
45793CB00001B/115